# PRAISE FOR
# *THE AI AGENT MANDATE*

"Essential reading on the division of labor in the era of AI."
—**Jay Bradner,** Chief Research Officer, Amgen

"A must-read for every executive seeking to
accelerate workforce productivity."
—**Ed Yardeni,** President, Yardeni Research

"The Future of Work is here with AI agents."
—**Steve Zabel,** CFO, Unum

"An essential road map to transform how work is
done between human and AI agents."
—**Michael Rafferty,** CEO, Rafferty Holdings

"Invaluable insights on how to deploy AI in the social sector."
—**Iqbal Dhaliwal,** Executive Director, MIT J-PAL

# THE AI AGENT
# MANDATE

## REIMAGINING WORK IN THE AGE OF AI

## MARCO BUCHBINDER

**FAST
COMPANY**
*Press*

Fast Company Press
New York, New York
www.fastcompanypress.com

This work is being published under the Fast Company Press imprint by an exclusive arrangement with *Fast Company*. *Fast Company* and the *Fast Company* logo are registered trademarks of Mansueto Ventures, LLC. The Fast Company Press logo is a wholly owned trademark of Mansueto Ventures, LLC.

Distributed by River Grove Books

Design and composition by Greenleaf Book Group
Cover design by Greenleaf Book Group and John Van Der Woude

Publisher's Cataloging-in-Publication data is available.

Print ISBN: 978-1-63908-111-0

eBook ISBN: 978-1-63908-112-7

First Edition

*To my beloved three sons, Marco, Massimo, and Matteo, who provide me daily inspiration and are my greatest and proudest life accomplishments.*

*To my parents, Franco and Franca, for their love, support, and sacrifices.*

*To my wife, Dana, for her love, encouragement, and tireless support of our family.*

# CONTENTS

# AI AGENTS DEFINED

AI agents are independent software solutions powered by advanced language models, Generative AI, machine learning, natural language processing and computer vision, robotic process automation, and analytics. They can comprehend context, learn from interactions, and carry out various tasks for users. These agents automate and streamline manual and/or document-intensive tasks—capable of scheduling, responding to inquiries, and even making decisions within set boundaries. They signify a move from passive AI tools to proactive, intelligent assistants that can participate in continuous conversations and adjust to user needs over time. AI agents, also known as "digital workers" or "AI assistants," engage with knowledge in a human-like, collaborative manner via an intuitive dashboard or voice commands. They are meant to work alongside knowledge workers, resulting in dramatically improved business efficiency and productivity. They may also be referred to as "digital assistants," though, as we will outline in this book, their ability to handle complex tasks, perceive their environment, make decisions, and take actions to achieve specific goals is what sets them dramatically apart from the single-task automation of today's digital assistants.

# PRELUDE:
# A MANDATE FOR CHANGE

*Progress happens when the context of the world changes so dramatically that the mandate for us to change is no longer optional.*

This is exactly where we find ourselves today, as a convergence of factors has made the adoption of AI agents and tools like ChatGPT an urgent imperative for staying competitive. Business leaders across all functions—from corporate strategy to talent management to digital transformation—must now understand how artificial intelligence will revolutionize work in the coming years. As we envision this future, it's crucial to shift our mindset about the workforce. The key to success lies in fostering collaboration between AI agents and human workers, not replacement. By positioning AI agents as partners that augment human capabilities, organizations can unlock new levels of productivity, innovation, and employee satisfaction.

If you're reading this, chances are you

- May want to understand how artificial intelligence, such as Generative AI and user tools like ChatGPT, will further change our businesses

- Are seeking answers to attracting and retaining talent and how AI agents can empower them

- Want to reduce your operating costs and/or find new revenue streams and see the potential for artificial intelligence to enable you to do so

- Are looking to manage and reduce your compliance risks

- Are a leader responsible for corporate strategy, oversee talent management for your organization, or lead a digital transformation effort

Whatever the case, I'm glad you're here.

Many factors led to the creation of AI agents, but progress is never just about one thing. Progress happens when the world's context changes so dramatically that change is no longer optional. Simply put, the liability of staying in the past far outweighs the risk of change.

That's exactly where we are today.

To fully realize the potential of AI agents, organizations must optimize workflows and processes holistically across the enterprise. Breaking down silos, realigning operations, and engaging workers at all levels to identify opportunities for AI to drive efficiency and innovation is key. This comprehensive approach lays the foundation for a thriving, AI-powered future.

In the pages that follow, I've explained in simple and unambiguous terms how critical AI agents will be in shaping the trajectory of your business's success and, more fundamentally, the future of work. This book is structured in a way that doesn't require you to read it from cover to cover. Instead, here are a few ways to read this book:

- You can easily skim through and pick up on the chapter previews, takeaways, and callouts that you're drawn to.

- You may dive into an individual chapter that piques your curiosity.

- You can read the book cover to cover or anything in between.

The following guide matches specific content you will find applicable to your role.

## Reader's Guide to This Book

Following are some hints on the sections that may be of most interest to you based on your role and areas of interest. Regardless of your specific needs, you will find the appendixes useful and informative.

You're a **CEO** or **business leader** who wants to understand how AI agents will alter your business and your industry:

- **Read Chapters 1, 2, 3, 4, and the Epilogue**

You're interested in the **technology** of AI agents and want to dive into how they work and are deployed:

- **Read Chapters 3, 4, and the Appendixes**

continued ⬎

You're a **CFO** or your focus is on **finances**, and you'd like to better understand how AI agents will impact productivity and the bottom line:

- **Read Chapters 2, 3, 4, and the Epilogue**

You're part of a small-to-medium-sized business and want to understand the competitive advantage of AI agents:

- **Read Chapters 2, 3, 4, and the Epilogue**

You are responsible for **human resources** and want to understand the impact of AI agents on your workforce:

- **Read Chapters 1, 2, 3, 4, 6, and the Epilogue**

Your focus is in **administration**, and you want to understand how AI agents will improve accuracy and efficiency as well as how they will change your workforce:

- **Read Chapters 3, 4, 5, 6, and the Epilogue**

You're the **COO** or your focus is on operations, and you want to know how to deploy AI agents:

- **Read Chapters 5 and 6**

You're like most of us and want to jump ahead and find out what the future will look like after AI agents:

- **Read the Epilogue and Appendix**

There are also various types of callouts in the book. You'll quickly grasp the type of information in each callout, based on its icon.

The compass icon represents guidance for the book, as well as chapter previews and takeaways.

The AI agent icon lets you know that the callout is about AI agents, their function, their value, or an area where they excel in amplifying your business.

The reading icon tells you to expect a use case or case study.

The information icon denotes a sidebar with research or other interesting insights.

# THE CORNERSTONES OF FUTURE WORK

As you read this book, it's important to keep five things in mind. I call these the Cornerstones of Future Work. They form the foundation for a hybrid, highly productive, amplified workforce composed of both AI agents and human workers. This may seem like a futuristic vision. It's already in action with early adopters and innovators.

1. The future of work is a **collaboration** between AI agents and knowledge workers.

2. AI agents **amplify** the abilities and creative contributions of knowledge workers.

3. AI agents **fuel innovation**, as they free our time from the demands of low-level work, so we can strategize and define new sources of value.

4. AI agents provide **greater productivity** with significantly lower costs.

5. AI agents **alleviate the burden of disparate, point technologies** from knowledge workers.

My goal with this book is simple: to build your understanding of AI agents so that you can effectively take advantage of what will be one of the defining transformations of the twenty-first century.

Thanks for joining me on this journey as we reimagine the future of work together. It may well dictate the difference between surviving or thriving in the age of artificial intelligence.

**—Marco Buchbinder**

# ACKNOWLEDGMENTS

I would first like to recognize Michael Rafferty, CEO of Rafferty Holdings and board member and investor at Ampliforce. I cannot say enough about our friendship and the support that Mike has provided me throughout my AI journey. He has been a believer from day one, and his guidance and support are immeasurable.

I would also like to acknowledge Michael Welts, CMO at Wasabi, marketing mastermind, and friend. Mike strongly encouraged me to write this book and was instrumental in helping me articulate my vision.

Finally, I would like to thank Rebel Brown, marketing expert, for her input and tireless efforts in keeping this book on track.

# INTRODUCTION

The adoption of AI agents is not optional: It's inevitable.

The impact will be felt by those who choose to adopt the technology, and equally by those who never adopt it. You can opt to not embrace these changes; the changes will happen regardless. As a case in point, think back to the introduction of the internet.

When the internet first came into being, the government brought it to life. Commercial organizations were not that interested. Boards of directors initially downplayed the value of the internet as part of their corporate strategy, partially due to concerns about information and intellectual property (IP) security. As businesses began to use the internet, it was as a tactical tool and without strong vision for its future.

Those who saw the future opportunity shifted their business thinking to encompass the opportunities the internet presented. Those companies are now among the brands we engage with every single day.

Today's advanced technologies will usher in transformation far beyond the internet. From sophisticated computations, predictions, and data analysis to the automation of complex processes, we are at the beginning of what may be the largest transformation ever driven by technology.

Yet this transformation, unlike past technology adoption, is also shaping what I am calling a Reimagined Future of Work. A future where knowledge workers, managers, executives, and others are liberated from various productivity challenges. This will in turn lead to the greatest productivity gains ever realized, greater job satisfaction, and higher retention rates.

In this reimagined workplace, it is my belief that 50 percent of the work done by today's knowledge workers will be done by AI agents within the next decade.

This productivity enhancement is not solely the result of Generative AI (artificial intelligence systems that can create new content, such as text, images, or audio based on patterns learned from existing data), although it is a significant contributor. Some see AI and related technologies as a move to replace workers. A different, more optimistic perspective is to focus on how the combination of these advanced technologies enhances workers' ability to do their jobs as well as take on additional higher-level work.

McKinsey research estimates that:[1]

- Generative AI alone could add the equivalent of $2.6–$4.4 trillion of value annually.

- Generative AI and other emerging technologies have the potential to automate 60–70 percent of current work activities, surpassing McKinsey's previous estimate that technology could automate half of employees' working time.

- Generative AI could boost annual labor productivity growth by 0.1–0.6 percent through 2040. When combined with other technologies, AI-driven automation could increase productivity growth by 0.2–3.3 percentage points annually.[2]
- It's clear that technology is poised to revolutionize the way we work once again, ushering in a new era of transformation.

> **As part of this shift, the potential of AI agents will not be nice to have; it will be a must-have.**

That's the essence of the AI Agent Mandate.
It's driven by the following factors:

- The diversity of technologies that are already impacting work in global business.
- The Perfect Labor Storm we are experiencing demands organizations and individuals to fundamentally reimagine work.
- Legacy business methods and beliefs that now limit our future growth and success.
- While we can't roll the clock forward, we can imagine what the future will look like.

## Imagining the Future of Work

The following table shares a few simple examples of how AI agents can and will impact our work lives.

continued ⬎

Just imagine how these fundamental abilities would impact your time and focus—and results.

| Role | Sample AI Agent Value |
|---|---|
| Business Leader | · Every morning, you receive relevant news summaries, competitive information, financial updates, and other insights that are mapped to your specific areas of interest. Your time can now be applied to higher-value work.<br>· You receive immediate summaries of meetings, key action items, and essential information. You easily track responsibilities and progress.<br>· Your AI agent continuously monitors incoming information and crafts appropriate responses or notifies you when you need to be involved. This minimizes tactical disruptions and distractions, freeing up time for high-value work. |
| Legal Team | · Your AI agent reviews legal documents and cases faster, identifies opportunities and issues, and makes decisions sooner.<br>· Your AI agent crafts legal briefs and filings, citing appropriate cases faster and in less time. The availability of accurate and complete case law increases the number of successful judgments.<br>· Legal teams receive daily updates on legal shifts or information that may impact your business. You know you have all the latest information, without using expensive legal resources to search for updates. |
| Human Resources | · AI agents orchestrate the hiring process, eliminating the high-volume overhead from HR professionals. HR can now onboard and process new hires with 10x greater efficiency and a 90 percent reduction in hands-on processing time.<br>· AI agents offer a more comprehensive analysis of employee metrics and data to better identify more opportunities and challenges.<br>· HR professionals have more time to create better employee experiences, drive higher retention, and increase productivity and engagement. |

| | |
|---|---|
| Contact Center | • Manual low-value tasks are off-loaded to AI agents. This creates 70 percent more opportunities for higher-touch interactions with customers and prospects.<br>• Contact center scripts and prompts are enhanced as AI agents learn, adapting to deliver the best possible customer interactions. Customers receive better experiences, leading to greater retention, new customer sales growth, and increased revenue.<br>• Thanks to dramatically reduced workloads for customer relationship management (CRM) updates, follow-up emails, and more, the contact center enjoys significant cost reductions from higher productivity, higher engagement, and less turnover. |
| Sales Team | • AI agents immediately update the CRM with customer insights, eliminating rep distractions from driving revenue.<br>• AI agents analyze a diversity of customer and prospect information to identify patterns and predict buying preferences and behaviors.<br>• Conversion rates increase as AI agents apply their analysis and recommendations, with human approval. The entire sales team's close rate benefits from continuously shared best practices to sales approaches. |
| Marketing | • Your AI agents analyze competitors to create highly differentiated product and positioning strategies.<br>• Your AI agents evaluate marketing and sales alignment and results to identify and create optimum campaigns for highly qualified leads.<br>• Your AI agents create personalized content for prospects and customers, increasing relevance, credibility, and engagement. |
| Employees | • Tedious, low-value, and repetitive tasks are off-loaded. Employee outcomes and productivity increase. Bottom-line results are amplified as employees focus on high-value skills to increase critical business outcomes.<br>• Employees are given the opportunity to develop advanced skill sets to deliver more satisfying, creative, and high-value work.<br>• Increased job satisfaction leads to enhanced employee retention, increased promotions, and career advancements. |

Why aren't we enjoying these benefits today?

One key reason is that companies have adopted hundreds of point solutions, with little regard to their seamless integration or impact on their overall functional processes. This has created a massive volume of mundane, repetitive, and frustrating tasks that distract us from the high-value work at hand.

Technology has delivered many promises. Yet, as we now know, the promises came with the burden of ever more disparate technology for human knowledge workers to support and stitch together.

According to a report from work management platform Smartsheet, "Automation in the Workplace,":[3]

- Over 40 percent of workers surveyed spend at least a quarter of their work week on manual, repetitive tasks, with email, data collection, and data entry occupying the majority of that time.

- Workers believe that automating these tasks will reduce wasted time (69 percent), eliminate human error (66 percent), and recover hours lost to manual, repetitive tasks that could be automated (59 percent).

- Nearly 60 percent of workers surveyed estimate they could save six or more hours a week—almost a full workday—if the repetitive aspects of their jobs were automated.

> Simply put, we have strapped a technology millstone to the necks of our most valuable human assets, knowledge workers.

Consequently, our most competent, and expensive, workers are spending a significant portion of their time on the mundane work required to fuel our data-dependent, technology-driven businesses.

When we have qualified and capable staff spending their time on mundane tasks, we lose out on what they can do best: use creativity, empathy, leadership, and intuition to make decisions and move the company forward.

In short, humans have been the superglue that holds it all together—until now.

**AI agents can and will change this dynamic.**

As you read this book, you'll explore these challenges, how the future of work must shift, and just how valuable AI agents are, as well as concepts like the following:

- Why our current processes and workflows are unsustainable without AI agents
- The tremendous competitive benefits that AI agents create
- How and where AI agents will make significant inroads in every single industry

In short, you'll have a vision of how AI agents can free up your most valuable resource—your people—to do what they do best: use their inherent high-value skills to assure that your organization thrives—whatever the future brings.

# 1

# THE PERFECT LABOR STORM

## Chapter Preview

We are experiencing the "Perfect Labor Storm." We may point to the social restrictions brought on by the COVID-19 pandemic as the ultimate catalyst that changed the way we work. In reality, a number of factors are driving this powerful and transformative organizational shift.

We'll first explore this phenomenon and its impact on our workforce, answering the following questions:

- What is the Perfect Labor Storm? What caused it?

- What impacts are we experiencing from the Perfect Labor Storm? What other impacts can we expect in the future?

- Is the Perfect Labor Storm causing workforce disengagement?

- What should we expect in the future concerning quiet quitting? How can we motivate employees so that they don't quiet quit?

- How do different generations feel about work? What can we do to motivate the different generations?

continued ⬊

- How do we retain the experience and knowledge of aging workers as they leave the workforce?
- Why are knowledge workers overwhelmed by manual, repetitive tasks, and what can we do about it?
- How do we rethink our workforce, our organizations, and our future to accelerate bottom-line growth?
- Why are AI agents the ideal solution to the Perfect Labor Storm?

In the late fall of 1991, a massive storm hit the coast of New England and the Grand Banks of the Atlantic Ocean. This meteorological event, known as "the Perfect Storm," would be immortalized in the book and film by the same name.

What made the storm so unique and powerful was the combination of three large weather systems. Because of the storm's behavior and size, it was deemed a once-in-a-century event.

A similar confluence of workforce factors is creating a Perfect Labor Storm, one that will create transformational repercussions on how work will get done.

# THE PERFECT LABOR STORM

It's hard to deny. We are at an inflection point regarding how we work, our labor force, and optimally leveraging our diverse technology.

We are experiencing the Perfect Labor Storm, right now. Here are just a few of the characteristics of this storm:

- Hiring, managing, and retaining employees grows more difficult every day, compounded by the struggle to maintain the productivity demanded for continued growth.

- Workers are more disengaged, as they are forced to work on more low-level, unsatisfying tasks.

- Managers struggle to engage and motivate teams while simultaneously adding more and more work demands.

- Natural workforce changes through retirement and young hires are bumpier as newer generations take their seats in this era. Our next-generation labor force, a.k.a. Gen Z and Gen Alpha workers, has no tolerance for low-value, boring work. They are already disengaging from today's workforce. Either we adapt to empower them to focus on high-value work, or they may become our competition.

Welcome to the Perfect Labor Storm.

How did we get here? Let's look at the contributing factors.

## The Great Resignation

We are experiencing the highest turnover rates in history.

Burnout is a key cause. In a recent Microsoft Work Trends study, 48 percent of employees and 53 percent of managers report that they're burned out at work.[1]

The cost of the Great Resignation is staggering.

- The national average turnover rate in 2021 was 47.2 percent.[2]

- By 2030, the US is expected to lose $430 billion due to low talent retention. And it's not just a US phenomenon. China will lose $150 billion because of low retention rates.[3]

- A hundred-person organization with an average salary of $50,000 could have turnover and replacement costs of approximately $660,000–$2.6 million per year. It's easy to see how quickly the costs of turnover can increase.[4]

- Over four million Americans quit their jobs each month in 2022. Poor mental health is skyrocketing, partly evidenced by 70 percent of the C-suite having considered quitting to find work that better supported their mental health and well-being.[5]

The Great Resignation can be directly linked to the increasing administrative and technology burden placed on knowledge workers—people are exhausted from slogging through their tedious but mandatory operational work, on top of their knowledge work.

### Administrative Burden

Today, we all believe that technology enhances our organization's productivity. But we also have to keep up with it. New tools continue to emerge that outperform previous bests, entangling us in a web of e-tools aimed to make our lives easier and improve our productivity. At the same time, we are learning that the sheer volume of disparate and point technologies actually creates more work for our already overburdened workforce. In this light, we see that these tools don't actually lighten the load—they just shift it.

In a 2021 study of 247 business software applications reported in *Harvard Business Review*,[6] every product claimed to save staff time. While there's no doubt that organizations gain efficiencies in some areas through use of these tools, researchers observed that these same technologies also required significant manual tasks that burden the workforce.

For example, a shift toward employee "self-service," such as an HR portal, dramatically increased the burden on employees as they spent inordinate amounts of time managing their benefits and attempting to use the confusing portal software.

In another case, a software product or collection of collaborating workflow products dramatically increased employee manual work requirements as they switched between applications, transferred data, consolidated data from a variety of applications, checked data accuracy across these systems, created reports, updated the source data, and more.

This burden is reflected in research across the marketplace. For example, in a survey by Smartsheet, employees noted that they spend approximately 40 percent of their day doing repetitive manual tasks.[7]

We'll further explore the impacts of our technology burden on workforce productivity in Chapter 2.

## Gen Z and Gen Alpha

"Quiet quitting" is a term that describes employees who are fulfilling their job requirements but not taking initiative, working overtime, or volunteering for extra projects or responsibilities. They're present and performing at par, yet checked out. It's a softer approach than outright leaving a job.

Quiet quitting is most attributed to younger employees. Gen Z and Gen Alpha have far less tolerance for work that isn't leveraging their intellect, creativity, and passion.

Quiet quitting is the result of a variety of factors, including:[8]

- **Stress and burnout.** Nearly half of Gen Zs (46 percent) and four in ten millennials (39 percent) say they feel stressed or anxious at work all or most of the time. A Gallup study with the Walton Family Foundation found that less than half (47 percent) of Gen Z Americans are thriving in their lives—among the lowest across all generations in the US today, and a much lower rate than millennials at the same age.

- **Living paycheck to paycheck.** Over half of Gen Zs (51 percent) and millennials (52 percent) say they live paycheck to paycheck (up five percentage points among both generations since 2022).

- **Second jobs.** Forty-six percent of Gen Zs and 37 percent of millennials have taken on an additional part- or full-time job to relieve financial pressures (+3 percent versus last year for Gen Zs and +4 percent for millennials).

Despite their work pressures, nearly half of Gen Zs and most millennials say their job is still central to their sense of identity, second only to their family and friends.

## An Aging Population

A US Census report has noted that by 2038 "older adults are projected to outnumber kids for the first time in US history."[9]

This shift clearly has implications for businesses. There will be a massive wave of retirement, which has the potential to disrupt a company's ability to get work done.

As long-term employees leave the workplace, they take with them the immense amount of corporate knowledge they've acquired—knowledge that is usually undocumented and perhaps unknown to others. They also take deep experiential knowledge of how to simply get work done inside the organization and with partners, not to mention their individual insights into working with specific employees, partners, and customers.

We need a way to retain this knowledge within the corporation. AI agents provide that solution.

# A NOT-SO-HIDDEN CHALLENGE

As part and parcel of the Perfect Labor Storm, a new challenge has arisen: quiet quitting.

In a highly competitive job market, workers may not feel they can quit, even when their jobs do not match their need for stimulating, creative work. They quiet quit instead.

## Quiet Quitting Is upon Us

- In 2022, the *Harvard Business Review* identified a phenomenon, especially prevalent among Gen Z and Gen Alpha, known as "quiet quitting."[10]

continued ↘

- According to June 2023 Gallup data, most employees are already doing just that: 59 percent of 122,416 global workers say they're not engaged at work.

- Gallup estimates that quiet quitting costs the global economy an estimated $8 trillion, or 9 percent of the global GDP.

- In the same research, 51 percent of workers said they were looking for new jobs. Aside from increased pay, their top two priorities were improved well-being and opportunities to grow and develop.[11]

The concept of quiet quitting isn't new. We have seen it before under terms like "work to rule" and "malicious compliance."

Regardless of the naming convention, the problem is the same: the need for positive employee engagement.

We, as employers, don't have the resources to capture—and retain—the attention, engagement, and loyalty of these critical workers. It's time to

- Transform the nature of work to address the factors that contribute to silent resignations and to meet the needs of our knowledge workers, who primarily work with information rather than engage in manual labor. This is where AI agents excel.

- Shift our business thinking and approach to embrace our workers' concerns about our business, the nature of their work, and the value they perceive they bring to the organization.

- Reimagine the future of the workplace, including providing the work-life balance our next-generation workforce demands.

High rates of resignation and turnover, increased demands on workers to keep up with administrative software, high rates of quiet quitting, and the loss of older, high-level knowledge and highly experienced workers coalesce to cultivate the Perfect Labor Storm.

The Perfect Labor Storm, combined with the massive demands of our data-driven, technology world, is contributing to a dramatic shift in our workforce. Even as workers do more and more "work," high-value work and outcomes are diminished. Yet, we have a powerful potential solution in artificial intelligence—assuming we shift our thinking and leverage technology to solve these challenges rather than adding to them.

In the next chapter, we'll discuss how our constant tactical technology adoption, the Perfect Labor Storm, and the changing nature of work have further pushed productivity to a standstill.

## Chapter Takeaways

- The Perfect Labor Storm is the result of many factors, including the Great Resignation. It created a tremendous shift in the way we view our workforce and the future of work.

- Hiring, managing, and retaining employees grows more difficult every day. Workers are more disengaged and don't want to work on low-level, unsatisfying tasks. Productivity suffers in these conditions.

- Burnout is a key problem. In a recent Microsoft Work Trends study, 48 percent of employees and 53 percent of managers reported feeling burned out at work.

continued ↘

- Quiet quitting is upon us. According to June 2023 Gallup data, 59 percent of 122,416 global workers say they're not engaged at work. Gallup estimates that quiet quitting costs the global economy an estimated $8 trillion, or 9 percent of the global GDP.

- Our next-generation labor force has no tolerance for low-value, tedious work. They are already disengaging from today's workforce. Either we adapt to empower them to focus on high-value work, or we lose them, forever.

- A US Census report has noted that by 2038, "older adults are projected to outnumber kids for the first time in US history." As our most experienced knowledge workers age out of the workforce, this presents a significant disruption in preserving knowledge that powers ongoing productivity.

- These factors coalesce to form the Perfect Labor Storm. This storm, combined with the massive demands of our data- and technology-driven world, is contributing to an ever-increasing drag on productivity.

# 2

# PRODUCTIVITY AT A STANDSTILL

## Chapter Preview

We've deployed technologies in search of the promise of increased productivity needed to fuel growth. Yet, we continue to face a productivity standstill.

As you'll see, numerous research studies confirm the severity of our challenge. Today's knowledge workers focus on high-value work for less than three hours per day.

In this chapter, we'll discuss our productivity challenge and its fundamental causes, such as:

- Why are we still challenged to increase knowledge worker productivity and performance?

- How can we focus knowledge workers on high-value, creative work rather than the administrative tasks that consume more than 60 percent of their workweek?

continued ↘

- How do we equip our workforce of the future to handle the ever-increasing volume of administrative tasks created by our data-driven world?

- Management and employees have dramatically different perspectives on true workforce productivity. How do we resolve this disconnect?

- How do we reimagine work in light of automation and AI?

- The overarching question is: How can we harness our technology investments to fuel our knowledge workers' performance rather than overwhelm them with administrative work caused by the same technology?

# NEW ERA, NEW CHALLENGES

Technological advances, from the computer age's silicon chips to the internet to smartphones, have been game changers for how work gets done in the twenty-first century.

Unfortunately, we are now learning that our ample and diverse workforce technology brings a set of new challenges.

Technology has contributed to solving some of the economic, labor, and organizational challenges we face today. However, technology has also become a barrier to work rather than a facilitator.

The Information Age ushered in an era of immense change, new business models, and new jobs for knowledge workers.

It also had a counterintuitive impact on productivity. Nearly a quarter of a century later, we continue to see an ongoing attempt to increase knowledge worker productivity.

## Too Much Tedium

Well into the Information Age, we continue to look for ways that technology can increase knowledge worker productivity. This remains an organization's most significant challenge with its knowledge workforce.

Truly, we're asking them to be optimally engaged—within an environment that sucks the life out of them through an endless stream of required tedious tasks. We hire them for their brains and skills and then burden them with this tedium, even at the cost of their growing discontent.

Today's knowledge worker is deluged with distraction, administration, and interruptions. Here are but a few statistics that demonstrate the undue burden on knowledge workers today:

- A study by vouchercloud.com on the routines of 1,989 workers found that the average office worker was only productive for 2 hours and 53 minutes daily.[1]

- A similar study of 185 million working hours, conducted by RescueTime, found that the average knowledge worker was productive for only 2 hours and 48 minutes a day.[2]

- Asana's Anatomy of Work Index shared even more unsettling insights. Over 9,000 knowledge workers reported that 62 percent of their workday is lost to repetitive, mundane tasks.[3]

- In a study by Smartsheet, nearly 60 percent of employees expect that they could save six hours or more a week with basic automation.[4]

- It's becoming clear: Our knowledge workers spend time orchestrating the technology-driven tasks that drive our vast data-driven businesses.

## Email: A Productivity Tool Run Amok

The advent of email made it easier to communicate with one another.

Today's reality is that email reduces productivity in several ways, including:

- **Time spent checking email.** It takes an average of sixty-four seconds to return to work after checking email, which can lead to hours of lost productivity per day.

- **Distraction.** Urgent emails can cause distractions and stretch timelines, interfering with employee focus, reducing productivity, and forcing employees to work additional hours.

- **Wasted time.** Less than half of emails deserve our attention, and much of what we spend valuable time writing goes unread, leading to wasted time.

- **Stress.** Email can increase stress levels in multifarious ways, which leads to further employee disengagement.

Consequently, the average employee spends 28 percent of their time reading and responding to email, according to the McKinsey Global Institute.[5]

It's clear that while we communicate more easily by email, it does not readily translate into being more productive.

# NOT SEEING EYE TO EYE

Another factor complicating our productivity discussions is the disconnect between management and employees. Management sees the bottom line and demands higher productivity, while employees, overburdened by mundane tasks, say they have no more to give.

The Microsoft Work Trends Index evidences this chasm. As

shown in Figure 2.1, 87 percent of employees believe they are productive at work, yet only 12 percent of managers believe their team
is productive.[6]

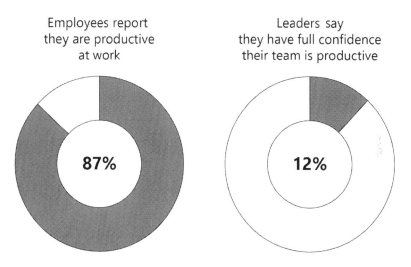

Figure 2.1 A Productivity Disconnect[7]

Throwing more and more technology at the problem isn't the
answer. We've done that for decades, increasing, rather than solving,
the overhead burden problem.

Any knowledge worker would welcome the prospect of a fric-
tionless forty-hour workweek—specifically, a job that allows them
to focus on high-value, interesting work rather than serving technological demands that stand in the way of getting their jobs done.

Unfortunately, that's not the direction we are going. In fact,
administrative and other bureaucratic tasks related to our widespread technology habits are increasing the burden on workers.

As you'll see in the following callout on health-care productivity, dealing with this bureaucracy requires hiring additional *administrative staff* to manage these technology-driven tasks.

## Health-Care Productivity at a Standstill

In health care, administrative knowledge workers have increased by a whopping 3,000 percent since 1970.

Yet, the percentage increase of actual clinicians has barely changed. Many of these people, including frontline workers, spend much of their time in an administrative quagmire.

For example, the typical doctor invests one hour entering and managing data for each hour they interact with patients. That easy math computes to 50 percent knowledge work and 50 percent admin work. The saddling of health-care workers with so much admin work is a major contributor to fatigue and burnout. Do you want your doctor burned out and tired or fresh and engaged?

In a 2018 survey of 6,695 physicians conducted by the Mayo Clinic,[8]

- 54.3 percent reported symptoms of burnout.

- Thirty-two percent reported excessive fatigue.

- 6.5 percent reported recent suicidal thoughts.

Physicians reporting errors were more likely to have symptoms of burnout, fatigue, and recent suicidal ideation. The increasing technological demands in health care, which often divert physicians' attention from patient care, have a cascading effect that ultimately diminishes the quality of care patients receive.

We can also thank increasing regulatory requirements in health care for the exponential increase in administrative overhead. The technological demands of these requirements are more likely the main contributor to the administrative burden.

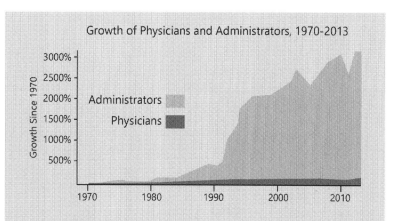

**Figure 2.2** Percentage Growth of Administrators and Physicians[9]

It is a small wonder that US health-care costs are exorbitant. For health care to focus on the patient over the administrative process, the health-care industry must drastically reduce or even shed these administrative burdens. Providers and payers can reallocate resources to improve patient outcomes and control health-care costs. In today's health-care system, this is nearly impossible for the patient to do independently.[10]

Health care is just one industry that fundamentally illustrates the magnitude of the problem that all industries face.

Workers are overburdened, administration has expanded, technology is seen as debilitating rather than facilitating, and customers often feel more frustrated by navigating different technologies, such as applications, data, and web pages.

> The sheer complexity and amount of work that knowledge workers are tasked with completing has expanded beyond the number of knowledge workers available to do the job.

We can change this trend by

- Empowering our knowledge workers to focus on high-value work by off-loading the volume of repetitive tasks demanded by our point technology expansion

- Simplifying our customer-facing technology into a seamless conversation to amplify the value of their interactions

- Implementing new approaches to manage the administrative burdens created by the very technologies we assumed would decrease overhead

As you'll come to see, AI agents are the ideal solution.

## PRODUCTIVITY IMPACTS OF AUTOMATION

Automation in heavily process-driven industries, such as manufacturing and financial services, has significantly impacted productivity. By streamlining processes, reducing labor costs, and tracking and analyzing data in real time, organizations have enjoyed enhanced success as simple tasks are off-loaded from workers.

However, when it comes to more dynamic and complex workflows typically managed by knowledge workers, traditional automation has not yet been able to match human capabilities. These nuanced processes often require adaptability and critical thinking that current automated systems struggle to replicate.

As a result, knowledge workers often find themselves trapped in a productivity paradox. They are primarily tasked with executing routine work rather than engaging in higher-level thinking and innovation. While they may appear busy and, therefore, productive, they are not contributing in the strategic, value-adding ways that companies truly need for growth and innovation.

Welcome to the productivity proxy.

# The Productivity Proxy

Noted economist Dr. Edward Yardeni discusses the concept of a "productivity proxy," which highlights a significant trend in productivity increases among nonfarm workers over the past seventy-five years. He observes that while productivity has dramatically increased, it is converging with GDP per payroll employee, indicating a trend of increased overall efficiency within the economy.[11]

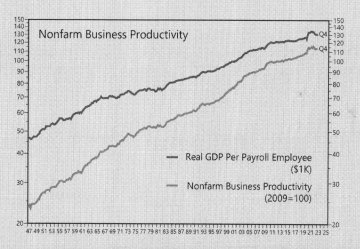

**Figure 2.3** The Productivity Proxy
Source: Yardeni Research, Inc.

This trend suggests that innovation, technological advancements, and other factors have led to higher output with fewer workers needed to produce it. In recent interviews, Yardeni shared his vision

continued ⬎

of productivity growth driven by "unprecedented technological advances [which are] laying the foundation for an era of economic expansion not seen in decades." He elaborated to Bloomberg News, stating, "I think productivity is going to make a comeback. There's robotics. There's automation. There's quantum computing. I think this is going to turn out to be something like the Roaring 2020s."[12]

# THE AUTOMATION GAP

Why hasn't automation been the nirvana we all expected? After all, automation isn't new. We've spent decades applying technology to automate human tasks in the following ways:

- We've automated the basic processes of our business flows using various tools and techniques.

- We've created vast islands of automation and disparate technology stacks that require increasingly greater assistance from knowledge workers to perform.

- We've automated work in place, yet we haven't approached automation as an opportunity to reimagine work and how we can leverage it to truly increase the productivity and engagement of knowledge workers.

## The Automation Gap

The straightforward way to differentiate early automation efforts from more robust efforts of AI agents is that early automation was deployed at the extreme ends of the enterprise, essentially creating islands of automation.

Early automation has been deployed in two distinct areas:

- Extremely large, cross-function implementations such as enterprise resource planning (ERP) for manufacturing and supply chains or customer relationship management (CRM) for sales, marketing, and support

- Discrete, specific, stand-alone tasks that automate a narrow process slice, such as a lightweight task-management system or macros built to work solely within a single app

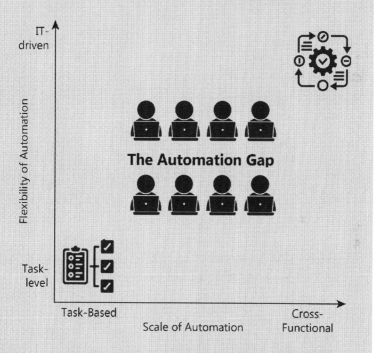

**Figure 2.4** The Automation Gap
Source: Ampliforce

Consequently, there needs to be more automation between these two extremes. Knowledge workers inevitably fill this gap, as shown in Figure 2.4.

continued ↘

This significant gap represents the bulk of activity still coordinated by knowledge workers. Much of the work in this space involves numerous handoffs between various applications, databases, workflows, documents, and workers. This represents the tedious, repetitive, yet logic-driven work where AI agents offer significant value.

## THE AUTOMATION WE NEED

It's obvious we need a better automation approach to off-load the volume of tasks created by our point technology and diverse automation approaches.

What do we need to move forward as the nature of work changes efficiently?

We need automation that has the following capabilities:

- Integrates across diverse systems and applications in a simple, background manner while delivering what knowledge workers need. Think of the power of business process management (BPM), a systematic approach to making an organization's workflow more effective, more efficient, and more capable of adapting to an ever-changing environment. It's a way to align business processes with an organization's strategic goals, design and implement process architectures, establish process measurement systems, and educate and organize managers so that they will manage processes effectively with the ability to consolidate information from diverse sources on-demand, as knowledge workers need, without the high IT overhead experienced with BPM.

- Intelligently and dynamically adapts to improve processes— without having to code or rewrite complex rules. Imagine robotic process automation (RPA) but elevated to a new level—one that can learn, adapt, and enhance efficiency across diverse systems and applications. This enhanced RPA would not only automate tasks but also conduct intelligent research, summarize findings, and even create content autonomously.

- Leverages the power of intelligent document processing (IDP) as part of a broader capability to ingest all information. To round out its capabilities, this innovative automation solution should harness the power of IDP as part of a comprehensive strategy to ingest and process all types of information. Think of IDP as seamlessly integrated into overarching, dynamic, intelligent search and automation abilities.

- Provides users with transparency, empowering them to explore comprehensive audit trails to document every single action, easily documenting compliance and regulatory requirements.

By combining these advanced technologies, we can create a truly transformative automation platform that empowers knowledge workers, streamlines complex workflows, and drives unprecedented levels of productivity and innovation in the modern workplace.

As we'll soon discuss, AI agents deliver these automation capabilities and more.

## Chapter Takeaways

- Investments in disparate technology and automation have yet to deliver the necessary productivity increases.

continued ↘

- In fact, our point technologies are vital contributors to knowledge workers' overload, distraction, and disengagement.

- The array of point technologies drives much of the overhead work, impeding productivity.

  ○ Study after study shows that knowledge workers lose around 60 percent of their workweek to repetitive, mundane tasks. It's causing burnout and discontent.

  ○ Knowledge workers are filling in for our automation gap. Early automation resulted in islands of automation at the task-based departmental level and cross-enterprise functional level, increasing the burden on knowledge workers to fill in the "gap."

- Owing to the proliferation of point technologies and the automation gap, knowledge workers are primarily tasked with doing rather than thinking. This is a primary driver of disengagement and "quiet quitting." It's also a key reason productivity is at a standstill.

- While workers might appear more productive because they're always working, they are not producing the outcomes companies need for growth.

- Throwing more and more technology at the problem only increases the problem.

- AI agents deliver the intelligent orchestration capabilities we need to solve the automation gap and amplify organizational performance. They directly increase knowledge worker productivity, engagement, and high-value outcomes.

# 3

# THE AI AGENT SOLUTION

## Chapter Preview

As we deploy artificial intelligence, we have the exciting opportunity to reimagine work.

What if we could blend the potential of artificial intelligence with the creativity and innovation of human workers?

Welcome to the world of AI agents. In this chapter, we'll explore the following topics:

- What are AI agents? What can AI agents do?

- Are AI agents like chatbots? Robots?

- Are AI agents hardware? Software? How are AI agents created? What's "under the hood"?

- How do AI agents automate the dynamic, complex tasks that we've failed to automate in the past?

- How do AI agents fill the automation gap?

- How do AI agents use artificial intelligence?

continued ⬎

- How do AI agents collaborate with and off-load knowledge workers? How do they communicate?
- How can AI agents improve your workflows and processes?
- Finally, we'll explore a case study where knowledge workers collaborate with AI agents in high-value, highly time-consuming processes.

# DRIVING THE MANDATE FOR AI AGENTS

As organizational leaders, we've dedicated years to the digital transformation of our organizations in pursuit of increasing market share and bottom line. Yet, we still haven't reached the next level of productivity, efficiencies, or profitability we envision.

The reality is that until we rethink the technology burden we place on our knowledge workers, process reengineering can only do so much.

We have reached a point when we must radically rethink the way knowledge workers and diverse, disparate technologies interact.

> What if we could blend the potential of artificial intelligence with the creativity and innovation of human workers?

> What if we could make work meaningful through technology rather than degrading work because of technology?

Enter the AI agent.

## What Do AI Agents Do?

AI agents are made from the latest AI and automation technologies and come fully configured to become part of your workforce. They complete tasks we ask them to complete based on how we train them.

Specifically,

- AI agents remove the distraction of repetitive tasks, empowering knowledge workers to do what they do best—think, innovate, and create value in new ways.

- AI agents do more than automate paper processes. They intelligently orchestrate knowledge worker processes, especially work that requires "intelligence." For example, they can read and summarize a document, review data from diverse applications and create a summary report, or perform a competitive analysis and create a sales tool summarizing key competitive advantages.

- AI agents collaborate as partners, interacting with knowledge workers to help them deliver better outcomes.

- AI agents learn as they work, offering insights and recommendations for improved efficiencies to their knowledge workers.

- AI agents capture every single action they do. This creates a transparent and comprehensive audit trail of every task and decision, which is critical for regulated industries and useful for all.

- AI agents provide accuracy without succumbing to fatigue and boredom. Humans begin to lose focus during long, repetitive tasks. AI agents provide the same diligence for the first five repetitive tasks as for the hundredth or ten thousandth repetition.

- AI agents can be used as "invisible tech," interacting directly with human workers to provide a seamless bridge for users as new/upgraded technologies or workflows are implemented. With the support of AI agents, knowledge workers don't need to learn a new set of skills or tools as business dynamics evolve or as point applications are upgraded.

- AI agents will communicate via advanced voice or other technologies as they collaborate with their knowledge worker partners. Just think of the way you interact with Alexa or Siri.

## What Are AI Agents?

AI agents are software that automates complex, dynamic workflows across diverse technology platforms and applications.

AI agents collaborate with human workers to off-load operational tasks, secure approvals, request input when new decisions need to be made, or conflicts emerge, and recommend enhancements to work or processes.

Indeed, AI agents are like professional assistants for their knowledge workers or other human employees.

Unlike chatbots and other simple automation, AI agents are highly intelligent, dynamically adaptive, user deployable, and fully transparent.

AI agents feature intelligence applied to orchestration, optimization, computations, analysis, and business logic. They can perform work that previously required human intelligence.

AI agents are also highly flexible and can be streamlined for a very specific process. The role of the AI agent determines what specific skills are included, and they can be expanded to automate complex, cross-application, and cross-data processes that require logic to complete.

How do they achieve this degree of competence and flexibility?

AI agents leverage a diversity of technologies, skills, and logic to perform their jobs. Each AI agent is created with the optimum capabilities they need to accomplish their specific role. When their role changes, additional capabilities can be added and/or in-place capabilities redefined.

## AI Agents: What's under the Hood?

Let's take a quick look at what's "under the hood" of a typical AI agent.

AI agents are composed of a wide array of technologies, skills, and business logic. Combined, they create dynamic, flexible, intelligent, and transparent automation.

**1.** AI agent technologies

AI agents use a variety of technologies to perform tasks and execute processes. The specific technologies to be integrated and how they are used depend on the role of each worker.

In general, key technologies include

- AI in the specific forms of Generative AI, machine learning, and natural language processing (NLP)

- Process automation, such as RPA and BPM

- Document processing, such as IDP

continued ↘

- Security layers
- Compliance layers

**2.** AI agent skills

Just as a human worker needs a specific set of skills to perform a role, so, too, do AI agents need specific skills to complete a process. Example skills include:

- Handling documents. Opening a document, reading a document, saving a document, printing a document, creating a new document, writing that document, etc.

- Using applications. Signing in to an application, operating the application, capturing information from the application, formatting and merging information across applications, and entering information into the application

- Using data. Finding data in appropriate sources, capturing, pasting, entering, saving, and analyzing data along specified criteria

- Prioritizing work. Understanding a list of tasks, prioritizing these tasks, and understanding critical path tasks

- Communication. Notifying a knowledge worker of events or issues around the tasks, escalating decisions to the knowledge worker, and communicating task completion

**3.** AI agent business logic

AI agents perform logical tasks as part of an overall process. The logic they execute depends on the workflow or task. For example:

- An AI agent can incorporate a specific set of logic rules that must be applied to a task or workflow, such as credit scoring in financial services. These logic functions are seamlessly integrated and executed at the appropriate steps within the overall workflow. For instance, in credit scoring, the AI agent might apply rules regarding income thresholds, credit history analysis, and debt-to-income ratios at various stages of the loan application process.

This integration allows for consistent application of complex decision-making criteria, enhancing accuracy and efficiency in financial assessments while maintaining compliance with established guidelines.

- AI agents can capture, analyze, and report on data using the same logic a human worker would apply.
- AI agents can also notify their knowledge worker partners when they encounter challenges, for example, when different logic is required, or when the rule they are following is in conflict with another rule.

The flexible nature of AI agents makes them straightforward to deploy for a wide range of workflows and tasks. As you'll see, the resulting productivity increases are compelling.

## Imagine . . . the Coming Workforce Shift

Imagine a typical organization without AI agents. In this scenario, the knowledge workers, represented by the icons in Figure 3.1, find themselves primarily focused on tasks of low strategic importance, such as process automation and process integration. These workers are trapped in a cycle of low-value work, with little time or opportunity to contribute to business innovation or process orchestration, which are critical for the organization's success.

continued ↘

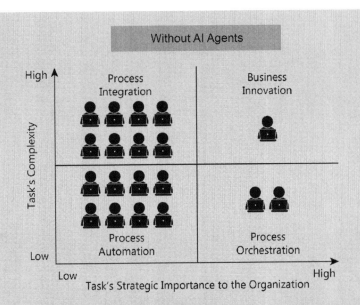

**Figure 3.1** Today's Workforce
Source: Ampliforce

Now, let's introduce AI agents into the workforce, as shown in Figure 3.2. These AI agents take over the majority of the process automation and integration tasks. This shift in responsibility frees up the knowledge workers, allowing them to allocate their time and skills to higher-value tasks that are of greater strategic importance to the organization. With AI agents handling the low-value tasks, knowledge workers can now focus on process orchestration, ensuring that the various processes within the organization are working together seamlessly and efficiently. Additionally, these workers can dedicate more time to business innovation, developing new ideas, products, and services that can drive the organization's growth and competitiveness.

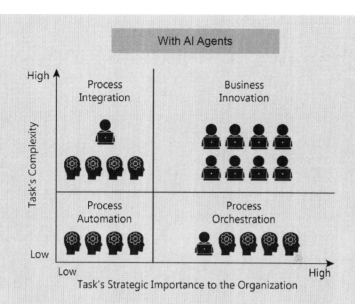

**Figure 3.2** Blended Digital Workforce
Source: Ampliforce

The introduction of AI agents enables a powerful transformation within the organization. By optimizing the allocation of tasks between AI agents and knowledge workers, the organization can unlock the full potential of its human workforce. Knowledge workers are empowered to contribute to the organization's success in more meaningful and impactful ways, leading to greater integration, orchestration, and innovation across the board.

In essence, the images illustrate how AI agents can revolutionize the way work is done within an organization. By leveraging the capabilities of AI agents, organizations can create a more efficient, effective, and innovative workforce, ultimately driving greater value and success in an increasingly competitive business landscape.

Let's now examine a simple case study to begin exploring the power of AI agents. This case study was conducted using internal customer-discovery calls at Ampliforce, the company I started in 2017 with the goal of applying AI to amplify complex business productivity and growth.

Through this research, we found that a human resources organization was struggling to streamline its hiring process. As a provider of enterprise-grade AI agents that amplify worker and business performance, fuel revenue growth, reduce worker costs, and simplify risk mitigation and compliance, Ampliforce focused on this case study to demonstrate how their AI-driven solutions can solve workforce productivity dilemmas.

## AI Agents and Hiring

**Before AI Agents**

Mary, our head of HR, needs to hire several senior software engineers. This involves the following tasks:

- **Identify candidates.** Mary manually searches recruiting websites for candidates. As she identifies the top hundred or so, she creates a spreadsheet for the IT hiring manager. Since different information is offered on each site, she normalizes the info for consistency. Where data is missing, she reviews each resume by hand. Mary also vets the candidates by reviewing criminal records, social media posts, and prior employers.

- **Send top candidates to the hiring manager.** Once she has her candidates identified, she applies weighting factors based on skills matches. She sends the top thirty candidates to the hiring manager for their weighting as well.

- **Interview scheduling.** After she has the hiring manager's ranking, Mary invites top candidates to interview. She also sends questions from the hiring team and requests a response. Mary then books the first round of interviews, coordinating the IT leadership team's calendars to find dates that include as many of the team members as possible.

- **Feedback and next interview.** After the first-round interviews, Mary summarizes feedback from the team for each candidate. She then ranks candidates and selects choices for final interviews. If she needs more candidates to fill the positions, she uses her initial list to find more candidates. She simultaneously schedules the final round of interviews for top candidates.

- **Hiring.** After the final round of interviews, Mary sends her recommendations to leadership based on their final rankings. After the hiring manager approves, she issues offer letters to the selected candidates. If a candidate rejects the offer, she goes to the next-highest-ranked candidate until all positions are filled.

Mary is driving this same hiring process for five to six groups in the company simultaneously.

## Mary's Unused Potential
After ten years with the company, Mary has a deep understanding of the company's culture and who best fits the culture; she can usually tell in a short interview who's a good fit and who isn't.

If she had more time to focus on filtering first-round interviews, she could save leadership hours and avoid back-and-forth communications.

The challenge? If she takes more time to do the first round of interviews, she won't be able to execute all other administrative parts of the process.

continued ↘

Let's now look at how an AI agent could amplify Mary's ability to improve hiring at her company.

**After AI Agents**

Mary hires an AI agent to off-load the frustrating research, paperwork, spreadsheets, scheduling, and other hiring tasks that distract her from her real job, finding and hiring the best candidate.

- Mary has the AI agent observing her to create the digital process map.

- She refines the map and then trains the AI agent.

- The AI agent connects with each of the corresponding datasets and apps via in-place APIs.

- The AI agent seamlessly off-loads the tedious manual systems work that is part of the hiring process. Specifically, the AI agent can take on the following tasks:

  - Identifying candidates. The AI agent reviews and finds candidates, creates the spreadsheet and rankings, and sends to Mary for review. Once Mary approves, the AI agents send the information to the hiring manager to add their feedback to the list.

  - Sending candidates to hiring managers. The AI agent handles all aspects of scheduling the interviews, collecting feedback, and ranking the candidates for final interviews.

  - Scheduling interviews. Candidates are easily scheduled, final feedback is collected, and the AI agents send it to all involved parties.

  - Hiring. Once candidates are selected, the AI agent collaborates with Mary to create and send offer letters, track responses, and set up newly hired employees for their first day in the office.

The AI agent engages with Mary in a conversational way whenever it encounters a task that it couldn't complete or didn't understand.

With her extra time, Mary now includes a "culture fit" interview at the beginning of each candidate's process, narrowing the field and saving management and team time.

The cost savings are significant.

Let's assume that there are seventy potential candidates and a fully loaded cost of $300K for Mary and each of the hiring teams in this example.

There is a total savings of $26,900 in process-driven hours for this specific hiring process.

Mary and hiring managers recover an additional 180 hours of time, thanks to the AI agent. This high-value time fuels more innovation and strategic opportunities.

This example depicts the value an AI agent delivers in a straightforward, common workflow process within our organizations.

By eliminating the manual, repetitive tasks and research time, the AI agent amplifies Mary and other leaders' time, empowering them to optimize the process, hire better candidates, and accelerate their workforce strategies.

I refer to the significant impacts that AI agents bring to our workforce and our organizations as the Amplification Effect. This amplification is seen in a variety of ways, from increased knowledge worker performance and engagement, to improved accuracy and productivity of operational tasks, to seamless technology integration as users require.

We'll discuss the Amplification Effect in the next chapter.

# Chapter Takeaways

We've invested significantly in the digital transformation of our organizations in pursuit of increasing productivity and bottom lines. Yet, we still haven't attained the level of productivity, efficiency, and profitability we desire.

AI agents offer a solution in our technology-filled, data-driven world.

- AI agents are neither robots nor chatbots. They are intelligent software that orchestrates complex, dynamic workflows across diverse technology platforms and applications.

- AI agents are composed of advanced technology, proven skill sets, and the logic your business uses to drive decisions. All are configured to meet your specific role's requirements.

- AI agents leverage artificial intelligence to execute work that requires "thinking"; for example, identifying market or competitive trends for an in-depth product analysis.

- AI agents learn as they work, expanding their knowledge and recommending changes to improve organizational processes, productivity, and outcomes.

- AI agents collaborate as partners, interacting with knowledge workers as needed to update work status, request direction or approval, seek additional information, and recommend improvements.

- In our case study, we saw how AI agents off-loaded volumes of mundane work in the HR hiring process to fuel cost savings, time savings, and improved candidate hiring.

- AI agents impact our workforce and our organizations in what I call the Amplification Effect.

# 4

# THE AMPLIFICATION EFFECT

## Chapter Preview

The Amplification Effect represents the added value that is realized as AI agents enter the workforce. It reaches far beyond amplifying human potential.

In this chapter, we'll explore its diverse impacts on your organization, answering questions including:

- What is the Amplification Effect? How does it impact my business?

- How do AI agents deliver the Amplification Effect?

- How does the Amplification Effect create an accelerating increase in overall productivity?

- How do the Amplification Effect and AI agents encourage and create opportunities for knowledge workers to focus on high-value work?

- How can the Amplification Effect accelerate future revenue growth and bottom-line profitability?

continued ◥

- How does the Amplification Effect increase the value of our technology and data in business operations?

- How will the Amplification Effect fuel creativity and innovation in our business thinking?

- How does the Amplification Effect increase the efficiency of our processes and workflows?

- How will the Amplification Effect improve our ability to meet regulatory compliance requirements with high accuracy and speed?

The Amplification Effect is the value an organization receives because of AI agents shifting the way we do work. As you'll see in this chapter, the effect is far-reaching. AI agents amplify human potential, organizational productivity, technology investments, responses to regulatory compliance, and our creative innovation, to name just a few.

## AMPLIFYING HUMAN POTENTIAL

Today's knowledge workers contribute to a work environment I call Knowledge Work 1.0. A variety of technology surrounds them, increasingly demanding more of their time to just feed the needs of the disparate technology.

In "Knowledge Work 2.0," technology is finally able to amplify human performance as AI agents augment the human worker. AI agents offer seamless integration and access to diverse technology systems, applications, and data, without the need for expensive IT-integration projects.

Knowledge workers seamlessly access the information they need through the AI agent, regardless of where it resides. The result is more accurate information and analysis in significantly less time, with far superior outcomes.

Consequently, Knowledge Work 2.0 will have ten times the impact on the global economy of its predecessor.

The required key element for this transformation to Knowledge Work 2.0 is the AI agent.

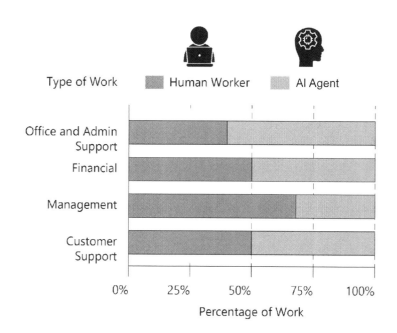

**Figure 4.1** A Collaborative Future
Source: Ampliforce

Let's look at the percentage of tasks in current job categories that could be assumed by AI agents.

In Figure 4.1 you can see the estimates for the percentage of current work that AI agents can accomplish. You can also see that the Future of Work is a collaborative effort between knowledge workers and AI agents.

As AI agents take on increasing amounts of tactical responsibility, their presence encourages and creates new opportunities for knowledge workers to do what they are hired to do—think and innovate.

This is a crucial point. As employers, we need to be sure that our knowledge workers understand that AI agents are partners, not threats. We'll discuss this more in Chapter 6.

## THE AMPLIFICATION EFFECT AND PRODUCTIVITY

Think of AI agents as coworkers that collaborate and amplify the abilities of human workers.

This new breed of employee radically alters the landscape of work. They usher in a new era of innovation by creating entirely new ways of empowering our human workers' productivity outcomes. They amplify the value delivered by knowledge workers.

# Amplified Productivity

The Amplification Effect creates accelerating productivity thanks to the collaborative capabilities of AI agents and their ability to infinitely scale when knowledge workers require more from them.

Figure 4.2 shares the expected impacts over time as AI agents enter our workforce.

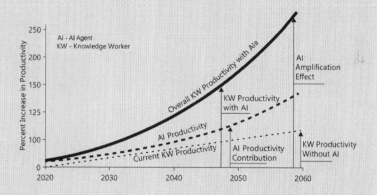

**Figure 4.2** The Amplification Effect
Source: Ampliforce

Based on its trajectory over the past forty years, we can expect knowledge worker productivity to increase by 1.5 percent year over year (light dotted line).

As AI agents take on more of the administrative work (dashed line), we expect a significantly greater increase in overall productivity of both knowledge workers and AI agents (solid line).

By 2050, this will account for at least a three-fold increase over currently projected productivity for 2050.

By 2060 the increase will be five-fold.

## Ongoing Process Optimization

AI agents also continuously optimize the processes that underlie human workers, further amplifying human performance.

As AI agents execute their work, they learn continuously.

Traditionally, we've used employee interviews to capture the details of the processes they execute, as well as their insights into what would improve these processes.

The challenge is that employees most often describe the process as they perceive it to be rather than how it actually works. This is simply human nature. As we become more proficient at work, we no longer have to think about what we do; we just do it. When people are asked about their jobs, they are not able to explain in full detail how they get their work done.

If we observe the work to document the process, the very act of observing is time consuming and not scalable. Observing people at work can also alter the way things are done, a phenomenon known as the Hawthorne effect.[1]

AI agents provide an objective perspective that eliminates human biases and delves much more deeply into how a process works. AI agents

- Observe human workers in their roles and document every action and decision.

- Use these insights to create a digital process map, which AI agents use for their training. (More on that in Chapter 5.)

- Explore and document larger, end-to-end processes, searching for a true picture of all variations in the process such as exceptions, bottlenecks, and errors.

- Recommend updates and changes to the processes to their knowledge workers, or managers, for approvals and implementation.

The result is continuously optimized processes that continue to amplify the value of our human workers and the outcomes they deliver.

# THE AMPLIFICATION EFFECT AND TECHNOLOGY

The Amplification Effect increases the value of disparate technologies. Thanks to this seamless integration, we'll have faster and better access, significantly reduced error rates, and the power to analyze information to predict opportunities as never before.

This amplification derives from the way that AI agents can interface and interact across information systems and technology.

> AI agents will become the interface for 90 percent of what we do today when we interact with technology.

## A Seamless Technology Interface

We have come to expect a unique application interface between ourselves and information systems:

- We take time to learn each distinct application interface we use.

- We flip screens between these interfaces without a second thought, hundreds of times a day.

- Just when we get comfortable using this version, a new version of the application or an altogether new application comes along.

- Once again, we are forced to learn how to use that application to do work.

- And we repeat this cycle, again and again.

Who among us hasn't experienced that moment of utter frustration when we ask, *What brilliant engineer thought that this was an intuitive way to use this application?*

We don't like it. We complain about it. Yet, we haven't had another option.

Until now.

AI agents will change this cycle. AI agents will become the interface for 90 percent of what we do today when we interact with technology.

In the same way that an executive of a Fortune 500 company has assistants to handle research, correspondence, financial analytics, and creating presentations, knowledge workers will have AI agents to interact with and use every technology they need to get the job done, without worrying about how to use the individual technology, applications, and related data.

You'll no longer need to know how to create and populate a spreadsheet, how to construct database queries to create customer analytics, how to determine the best way to format a presentation, or how to correlate data across different patient records to get a view of a patient's complete history.

Nor will you have to learn how to reuse the underlying applications at every update or upgrade.

The concept of an AI agent interface across applications is already in play. You experience it when you interact with ChatGPT, Bard, or other GenAI systems. You don't need to know how to search the web, write code, or design an app to achieve the outcome you want. What you do need is the creative wherewithal to know what to ask and the expertise to use the results to create value.

This is only the beginning of the value of AI agents, unleashed.

## Amplifying Workforce Technology

We see the proliferation of point technology and its productivity impacts across numerous industries. Let's look at an example.

In the following graphic, you can see the wide range of point technologies deployed in a typical enterprise today. While some integration exists, we all experience the frustration of copying and pasting data from multiple application screens into a spreadsheet or document for analysis and reporting. We also experience the frustration of being unable to combine information from diverse sources into a single view without significant manual work.

Each of the application types on the left represents a typical layer of operational data and processes within and across an enterprise.

As you can see in Figure 4.3, each of these technologies also adds another layer to the "technology stack" for knowledge workers to manage.

As each technology was added, the volume of tasks increased as well as the complexity of managing the additional data demands from knowledge workers.

continued ⬊

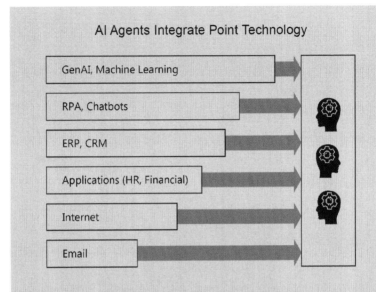

**Figure 4.3** Seamless Technology Integration
Source: Ampliforce

AI agents solve this challenge by introducing an orchestration layer that buffers the knowledge worker from the diversity of the point technology stack. This serves to integrate diverse data without the IT overhead associated with full-scale integration projects.

AI agents deliver integrated data as knowledge workers need, giving them the most accurate, comprehensive information possible. Knowledge workers can then apply their innate intelligence and experience to analyze, report, and otherwise use this information for creative, high-value work.

# AMPLIFICATION AND RISK MITIGATION

The advent of regulatory compliance added tremendous demands on our organizations. The time and cost implications are significant.

When it comes to time spent, Drata Research shared research showing the following:[2]

- 25 percent of organizations spend less than 1,000 hours on compliance a year.

- 35 percent spend 1,000–4,999 hours.

- 20 percentspend 5,000–9,999 hours.

- 20 percent spend over 10,000 hours on compliance a year.

NorthRow, a compliance software provider, researched the cost of compliance. They found that[3]

- On average, 25 percent of business revenue is spent on compliance costs.

- 18 percent of businesses estimated that more than 50 percent of revenue is spent on compliance costs.

- While there are compliance-focused tools designed to support compliance audits, NorthRow research found that 40 percent of compliance teams use basic productivity tools such as word processors and spreadsheets to run processes.

As you can gather, compliance is a significant contributor to the mundane administrative tasks faced by knowledge workers.

## Comprehensive Auditing Amplifies Compliance

AI agents continuously monitor and track processes as part of their role. AI agents record every detail of their work, including actions, data access, and the logic they use to make decisions.

This creates a comprehensive audit trail that supports compliance tracking and documentation, off-loading volumes of work required to create such detailed audit documentation.

> **AI agents bring the power of Generative AI to highly regulated organizations.**

AI agents provide complete transparency, unlike Generative AI. Current GenAI tools are "black box" in nature, meaning they do not offer transparent views into actions taken, data accessed, or the logic behind decisions or model training. Consequently, GenAI cannot provide the documentation and tracking needed to satisfy compliance requirements.

By providing comprehensive audit capabilities, AI agents bring the power of Generative AI to regulated organizations. In fact, according to research from IT company Accenture, 93 percent of compliance teams agree that new technology like artificial intelligence and cloud software will make compliance easier.[4]

# THE AMPLIFICATION EFFECT AND INNOVATION

We all know we need to allocate more time to focus on strategy and innovation. Yet we seem to spend less and less time doing just that. It's an ongoing trade-off between running the day-to-day business and looking toward the future.

AI agents fuel innovation that will inevitably lead to business growth and the creation of new industries. These advancements will employ far more human workers doing more productive and enjoyable work as the bottom line grows.

It's also clear that executives recognize the value of innovation. For almost half of the 1,757 executives PWC interviewed (43 percent), innovation is a "competitive necessity" for their organization. In five years, that figure increases to 51 percent.[5]

## The Innovation Puzzle

It's clear that innovation is a key factor in business growth. A recent PwC report[6] *Breakthrough Innovation and Growth* highlights the crucial role of innovation in driving corporate growth and provides insights into what separates the top innovators from the rest. According to the report, over the past three years, the most innovative 20 percent of companies surveyed achieved 16 percent higher growth compared to the least innovative 20 percent. Looking ahead, these innovation leaders expect their growth to accelerate to nearly double the global average and three times that of the laggards over the next five years. For the average company, this equates to approximately $500 million in additional revenue over the five-year period compared to less innovative peers.

However, achieving breakthrough innovation is not easy. The PwC study identified several key challenges companies face, including rapidly commercializing ideas, attracting top talent, building an innovation culture, and finding the right external partners.

To overcome these hurdles and drive successful innovation, the report recommends a holistic approach that encompasses many aspects of the business. This includes aligning innovation strategy with overall corporate goals, fostering leadership commitment and innovative culture, securing the best talent, collaborating with external partners, implementing effective innovation processes, managing

continued ↘

a balanced innovation portfolio, establishing proper governance, dedicating sufficient funding, and measuring innovation performance.

In today's business environment, innovation is no longer optional but a strategic necessity that will determine the growth leaders in the coming years. Companies that can crack the innovation puzzle and systematically embed innovation across their organization will be well positioned to outperform their peers and achieve breakthrough growth.

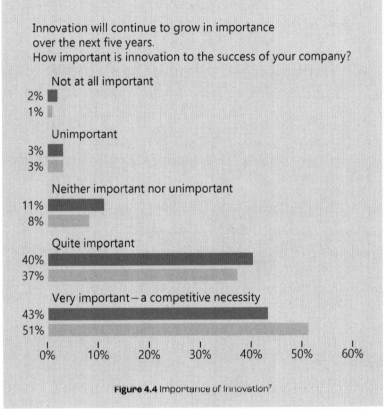

Figure 4.4 Importance of Innovation[7]

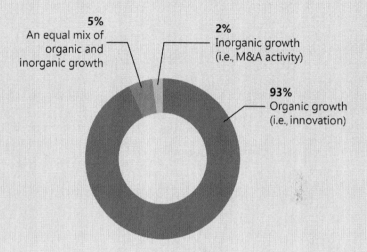

**Figure 4.5.** Growth Drivers[8]

These same leaders recognize the material impact innovation has on their revenue growth opportunities. In fact, they believe that innovation will drive a significant majority of revenue growth.

Still, the time we spend on innovation and strategy continues to decline. According to a 2021 survey by McKinsey, the average amount of time spent on innovation by executives has decreased significantly over the past few years, from 6.7 percent of their workweek in 2015 to 4.7 percent in 2020.[9]

While innovation remains a priority, business leaders are facing increased pressure to find time and resources to dedicate to innovation.

Given our current productivity trends, we face a continuing decline in the time available to focus on strategy, unless we change the way we accomplish day-to-day work.

We recognize the value of innovation. So why do we still struggle to dedicate time and resources to the creative explorations that drive that innovation?

One of the limiting factors is the productivity dilemma we all face. Whether you're a leader, a manager, or a knowledge worker, your time is consumed by the day-to-day tasks, interruptions, and distractions that are part of work today.

By amplifying the innovation potential, AI agents accelerate your future revenues, growth, and bottom-line profitability.

Just imagine: What would you do with significantly more time to explore new opportunities or markets for your business? Or spend more time with your customers?

## AI Agents' Power Innovation

In this example, we'll examine how a traditional health insurance marketplace leveraged AI agents. The result was a shift in business models to deliver a much more customer-experience-focused, digital-savvy business model via an online marketplace.

**Before AI Agents**
Buying health insurance through an online marketplace was handled by licensed insurance brokers or by a customer using a self-service capability.

The marketplace offered a front end that provided plan information to brokers and customers. Yet all questions, quotes, applications, acceptances, policies, and payments were handled by human workers.

This created a massive increase in the volume of manual work, which was normally handled by hastily trained data-entry temps.

High percentages of work done by temporary workers were found to be incorrect, triggering rework and cleanup, as well as negative social media posts and plummeting customer satisfaction scores, and creating irate clients and carriers.

The entire process to initiate a new insurance policy took seven business days or more.

Even as new policy revenue held steady, margins for the business continued to diminish, mostly due to the voluminous workloads created by the diverse systems and application process. Executives were so busy managing all the additional workflow and process tasks that they lacked the time (not to mention capital) to search for ways to improve.

**After AI Agents**

The company hired AI agents to streamline their existing processes in a lightweight, cost-effective way. Since AI agents seamlessly leverage existing systems, there was no need to make a significant investment for IT integration.

They hired a set of AI agents to off-load the policy application, review, acceptance, payment, and issuance processes.

- A **knowledge-analyst AI agent** extracts, reads, understands, and creates rules based on the documentation from each carrier and the state regulatory body. This information creates the digital rules implemented within the marketplace itself. The worker also updates these rules continuously.

- A **conversational AI agent** answers questions from clients and employees. It continuously ensures that answers are consistent based on current law versus workers' memories.

- A **process-analyst AI agent** analyzes the tens of thousands of transactions executed each year, providing recommendations for optimization.

- The **process-analyst AI agent** also created a digital repository of scanned archived images, PDFs, and emails of past

continued ↘

transactions. The marketplace now automatically processes 95 percent of the documentation without human intervention, including flagging errors that trigger notifications to clients.

- An **enrollment-processing AI agent** orchestrates the handoffs between knowledge worker teams, performs data entry, and rekeys data, eliminating manual data entry. Exceptions that require a supervisor are immediately flagged for action with the appropriate party.

- A **payment-processing AI agent** ensures that enrollment and payment systems reflect the same data and status of any given account. This eliminates the need for human rekeying of payment notifications via email or SMS messages for updates, payment confirmations, and payment issues.

- An **intelligent interface** driven by an AI agent now interacts with direct marketplace customers. The AI agent guides them through the application, including submitting supporting documentation.

Thanks to AI agents, the marketplace eliminated the need for temporary workers, reduced data-entry errors, and mitigated the stress overload for their knowledge workers.

The budget savings from eliminating backlogs and rework was redirected toward training customer service employees with consultative skills. This enabled more proactive outreach and relationship building to retain customers, reducing customer churn.

### The Marketplace Innovates

Now that daily operations have been streamlined, executives and their teams have the time and energy to brainstorm, identify, and pursue new opportunities. They also use AI agents as part of this innovation journey. AI agents research, analyze, and recommend opportunities based on competitive insights cross-mapped to consumer trends. These same workers also research complementary offerings in ancillary markets, seeking new revenue opportunities.

These recommendations formed the baseline for teams to step outside the box to creatively explore and define specific new opportunities to increase revenue, reduce costs, and manage the compliance demands of the insurance industry. The results were

- **New revenue opportunities.** Customer satisfaction, reviews, and referrals dramatically increased as AI agents accelerated and simplified the tedious insurance processes. As a result, the company grew in the number of new policies issued, as well as current policy renewals. The company began to cross-sell related insurance products to their now happy customers.

  Thanks to the AI agents' research and analysis, they were able to identify a suite of secondary offerings, then map each to the profile of individual customers. The AI agents created personalized offers for these customers when they used the portal. The offers were delivered on the marketplace with succinct customer focus, noting why the customer would want the offer and its specific value to that individual customer.

  Revenues and margins continued to grow.

- **Reduced costs.** The initial deployment of AI agents offered cost savings, as the requirement for hiring and training temporary data-entry employees was eliminated. Additional knowledge workers and AI agents were added to support the increase in policies handled, resulting in the continued decline of cost/policy and an increase in margins.

- **Regulatory compliance.** Governed by a range of federal and state regulations, insurance companies must ensure consumer protection. Previously, documenting every step of every policy's process required significant overhead, had to be manually created across diverse point systems, and was prone to errors. AI agents track and document a comprehensive audit trail of all actions.

*Source: Ampliforce*
*Be sure to review the case studies in the Appendix to explore specific quantitative impacts of AI agents.*

As you can see, the Amplification Effect has tremendous potential to shift the way your organization works, your workforce performance, and the bottom-line results you'll enjoy.

By now, you're wondering what it takes to deploy these workers to amplify your own workforce and organization.

We'll cover that in Chapter 5.

## Chapter Takeaways

AI agents improve productivity and performance outcomes, which amplifies the value of your organization with increased productivity, performance, accuracy, and technology while accelerating innovation.

- The Amplification Effect is not simply a linear increase in overall productivity. It delivers an *accelerating increase* due to AI agents' collaborative capabilities and their ability to infinitely scale as we require more from them.

- As AI agents take on tactical work, they *amplify new opportunities for knowledge workers to accomplish high-value, creative work.*

- As AI agents monitor and audit their work, they also continuously learn to dynamically optimize processes, *amplifying* ongoing efficiency.

- AI agents usher in a new era of innovation by *amplifying* time spent on creative and innovative work.

- The Amplification Effect can also be seen in the *increasing value of our disparate technology.*

- AI agents *amplify our ability* to use critical business information. I expect them to become the interface for 90 percent of today's technology interactions.

- AI agents *amplify* our accuracy and speed in responding to regulatory compliance requirements by delivering comprehensive audit documentation.

- By *amplifying* our business productivity, performance, efficiency, and time spent in innovative work, AI agents decrease costs, increase revenue, and fuel bottom-line growth.

# 5

# DEPLOYING YOUR AI AGENTS

## Chapter Preview

In this chapter, we'll focus on taking our firsthand experience with customers and the pain points they are looking to solve with the application of AI agents at Ampliforce. Deployment of AI agents is a major topic; specifically, customers want to know:

- How do I deploy AI agents? Do I need IT to deploy AI agents?

- What types of work do AI agents do? How do they perform their work?

- How do I decide which projects are best to assign to an AI agent?

- What is a digital process map, and how do I use it? How does it help me better deploy and use my AI agents? How do I train my AI agents?

- How do AI agents navigate the systems and data they need to use, understand the rules they must follow, and identify their next tasks?

continued ↘

- What is the supervisory role of Humans in the Loop (HITL) with AI agents? How do AI agents know when to request input from their human workers?

- How do knowledge workers and the organization manage AI agents in day-to-day work, as well as measure their efficiency and accuracy?

- We'll close with a financial services case study, featuring the value of AI agents in a research-intensive financial services workflow.

Let's begin by addressing the questions that customers ask about AI agents, their training, their work, their interactions with humans, and their ongoing management.

# KEY QUESTIONS ABOUT AI AGENTS

Following are the key questions most customers ask when we discuss the value of AI agents in their business:

- What processes will AI agents be executing?

- How does my business document what those processes are?

- How are AI agents trained on those processes?

- How do AI agents know which systems they need to use?

- How do AI agents know the rules they need to follow?

- How do AI agents know where to find their next task and what that task is?

- How do AI agents know when they don't know enough and should involve a knowledge worker?

- How will I know that my AI agents are working?

- How do AI agents do their work?

Let's begin.

## What processes will AI agents be executing?

Just like human workers, your AI agents need job descriptions that clearly define their responsibilities and work they are to accomplish.

For instance, an insurance policy processing clerk AI agent is responsible for processing applications for, changes to, reinstatement of, and cancellation of insurance policies. This includes mundane tasks such as

- Reviewing insurance applications to ensure that all questions have been answered

- Compiling data on insurance policy changes

- Updating policy records to match the insured party's requests

- Canceling insurance policies as requested by the insured or due to lapses in payment or other business rules

- Reinstating policies once payment has been reestablished

While existing job descriptions are a starting point, they do not fully articulate how this work is accomplished. In other words, we need to fully understand every step and action in the previously listed tasks, including the entire workflow, data sources, and how each step in the process is handled.

> By clearly defining the role of the AI agent, organizations can ensure they are leveraging these powerful workers to their fullest potential.

It's also important to note that AI agents are capable of work far beyond mundane tasks. AI agents can execute creative and complex tasks. As AI agents learn and integrate more with their knowledge worker partners, their potential expands, which means your team can expand their roles beyond their initial focus.

Clearly defining the role of the AI agent today ensures that you are leveraging them to their fullest potential. As their role expands, you can continue to document their responsibilities easily using the following digital process map.

### How does my business document those processes?

Think of AI agents as a new kind of employee, filling an open job position. As the hiring manager, it's important to define the processes involved, step by step, to provide a clear map for the AI agent to follow.

In the early days of expert systems design, developers interviewed and observed experts doing a particular job to replicate their expertise in a systemic way. Nonexperts could then achieve a higher level of work by using these systems, thus making them "experts."

We use the same baseline approach to define a digital process map. Yet we have an advantage in creating an even more detailed, informative map by integrating a business-process AI agent with process discovery tools.

This business-process AI agent observes a human worker document a role, essentially becoming an "expert" at the specific workflows you need. The AI agent then creates the digital process map to be followed by the specific AI agent for that role.

## The Digital Process Map

Digital process maps are essential tools that describe how a series of tasks are performed within a workflow. These maps provide a layered approach, allowing you to drill down into more specific actions and targets as needed, similar to how Google Earth enables you to zoom from a whole-earth view to a street-level view.

In the following example, an AI agent observes a knowledge worker processing a claim and creates a detailed digital process map. This map includes several key components that enable the AI agent to learn and effectively execute its role:

- Process overview (Figure 5.1): This high-level view outlines the main steps in the workflow and the specific tasks included in each step. It provides a comprehensive picture of the entire process from start to finish.

- Detailed task breakdown (Figure 5.2): This deeper layer of the digital process map delves into the specifics of each task, providing a granular set of steps that the AI agent must follow to complete the work accurately and efficiently.

- Rich, example-based learning: As the AI agent observes the knowledge worker performing the tasks, it gathers numerous examples of how the work is done. This wealth of real-world data serves as a comprehensive baseline, ensuring that the AI agent has everything it needs to learn and replicate the role effectively.

continued ↘

By leveraging the digital process map, the AI agent can quickly and effectively learn the intricacies of the role it is designed to perform. This detailed, layered approach enables the AI agent to understand the workflow at both a high level and a granular level, ensuring that it can execute the tasks with the same level of accuracy and efficiency as a human worker.

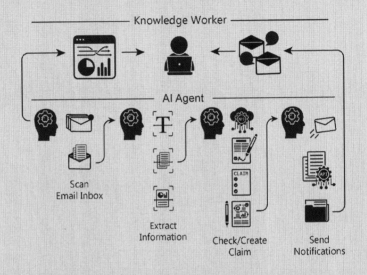

**Figure 5.1** Digital Map of Collaboration between Knowledge Workers and AI Agents in Insurance Claims
Source: Ampliforce

The process of creating a digital map is also valuable for the organization. The process documents the organizational environment, processes, and how people work within it. This empowers consistent training of both the AI agent and knowledge workers. You also provide both employees and leaders with a better understanding of the organization and its processes. Digital process maps also serve as audit tools, ensuring that the process is executed correctly.

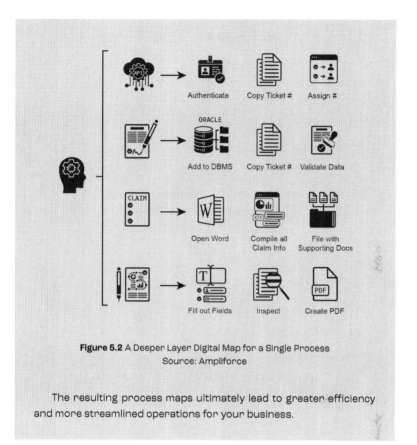

**Figure 5.2** A Deeper Layer Digital Map for a Single Process
Source: Ampliforce

The resulting process maps ultimately lead to greater efficiency and more streamlined operations for your business.

## How are AI agents trained on processes?

You hire an AI agent based on the specific skills you need, just as you'd hire a knowledge worker. Then, as you'd train a human worker, you'll train your AI agent on your specific requirements.

For example, an AI agent will have pre-selected skills that match the requirements of an insurance policy clerk. You simply train them to align with your specific business rules and procedures. AI agents then provide specific skills, applied to your specific workflows.

The training is straightforward:

- The digital process maps are uploaded to the AI agent.

- The AI agent's existing knowledge and skills are merged with the unique nuances of your organization's processes.

- AI agents are now ready to seamlessly integrate into your business, as you specifically need them to work.

## How do AI agents know which systems to use?

The digital process map trains your AI agent to access the systems and data it will use to execute its responsibilities.

As part of hiring your AI agent, the appropriate accounts for each system must be set up, just as access must be granted for a human worker.

## How do AI agents know which rules to follow?

The digital process map also captures your organization's specific rules that the AI agent must follow.

Typically, you will identify a digital knowledge base, or the digital standard operating procedures (SOP), documentation that a knowledge worker refers to during their work. The same queries and logic are then implemented by the AI agent, with additional guidance on what constitutes the "best choice" in terms of data that results from searches. These rules are also included in the AI agent's training.

Human workers can be included as checkpoints or for approvals within the process, a feature known as Humans in the Loop (HITL). For example, AI agents in regulated industries may very well have numerous checkpoints with their knowledge worker partners to assure full compliance or to make critical decisions.

More complex rules can also be defined and applied, offering intelligent logic to make decisions or choose next actions as part of the overall workflow.

### How do AI agents know where to find their next task and determine what that task is?

The digital process map is instrumental in defining the work queues that AI agents follow, along with the rules that dictate how to prioritize tasks. Prioritization rules can be based on various factors, such as the age of the task, priority tags assigned to certain tasks, regulatory needs, escalations, or other schemes.

By leveraging the digital process map in this way, organizations can ensure that AI agents are able to effectively navigate the queues and prioritize tasks based on the specific rules and criteria established by the organization.

## How do AI agents know when to include a knowledge worker?

Human workers routinely deal with contingencies and ad hoc situations that require case-by-case decisions or seeking higher-level inputs to resolve. Experts are brought into the loop to make decisions when the rules no longer suffice or next steps are unclear.

AI agents will encounter requests that they are unsure how to handle, or that require authorization from a manager. The rules governing these events are documented in the digital process map; for example, when and how to escalate, to whom it should escalate, which queue or communication channel to use, and what to do if the task is assigned back to the AI agent.

By incorporating these rules into the digital process map, organizations train AI agents to effectively navigate complex or unexpected scenarios. The escalation process is optimized, resulting in faster resolution times and improved overall efficiency.

## How do I know that my AI agents are working?

You'll want to monitor and validate the efficiency and accuracy of AI agents periodically.

You can remotely observe the AI agent's screen, which can be likened to watching over the shoulder of a knowledge worker. The AI agent's activities can be monitored in real time. For example, you can check in as AI agents move between applications, look up information, choose options from menus, and perform calculations.

For the instances where AI agents directly integrate into systems versus using a screen interface, a dashboard can track key metrics relevant to the work being done. Examples of such metrics include throughput, average processing time, flow of work from one AI agent to another, bounce rates when work is diverted to knowledge workers, critical time metrics to process tasks, and accuracy or audit metrics.

Hiring AI agents also provides an opportunity to reevaluate key performance metrics. It's a perfect time to consider how to measure productivity based on outcomes versus outputs, as well as how the AI agent is enhancing efficiency and creating new opportunities for creative work from knowledge workers. We discuss this in more detail in Chapter 6.

### How do AI agents do their work?

AI agents use three main categories of skills to perform their work: understanding, deciding, and acting.

Each of these categories depends on a variety of technologies, skill sets, and logic.

## UNDERSTANDING

AI agents identify, extract, and transform data into a digital format that they can use and understand.

## DECIDING

Once the data is in digital format, AI agents determine the next steps to take.

For example, an AI agent processing large amounts of data may use machine learning to discover patterns in that data that are required to make accurate decisions.

## ACTING

AI agents use automation and AI tools to perform specific actions, such as copying and pasting information between systems, submitting data for processing, and generating content for internal or external use.

Now that we understand more about how AI agents operate and the technical skills they use to do their job, let's explore an example of AI agents in action.

### Amplifying Asset Management

A global investment firm's fund-management team was planning to expand market share in the registered investment advisor (RIA) segment, both in terms of new customer acquisition and existing account growth. The team decided that a Digital Workforce could accelerate, support, and de-risk their effort to yield the highest ROI and measured effectiveness possible.

The team started by identifying the key opportunities in their sales process where the AI agents offered promising solutions. Some specific challenges included the following:

- The asset manager's business analysts spent significant and costly time researching market data to review the key market trends and identify major actionable themes.

- The business analysts then worked with the portfolio managers to determine the expected best performing funds that aligned with the identified key market trends.

- The marketing team would then send a series of analysis reports to all the sales representatives, highlighting the funds with the highest performance potential. Portfolio-management indicators were also included in the report.

- The strategies and metrics drawn from the research and trend analysis offered powerful sales insights, but they weren't used effectively by the sales team. The reps had to synthesize volumes of diverse information, resulting in inconsistencies in how the insights were applied to promote the funds, which led to different clients receiving different insights.

- There were issues regarding compliance, specifically concerning the information that sales reps sent to RIA prospects. The organization needed better controls to meet compliance demands, including messaging templates and a tighter approval process.

The sales processes were not yielding the desired revenue, cross-selling, and new-customer-acquisition goals. Additionally, these processes were not well tracked, nor were they analyzed to improve their effectiveness.

**After AI Agents**

The team implemented AI agents to increase assets under management (AUM) and drive greater fund inflows. They created digital road maps for the AI agents to streamline and enhance the outcomes for the company. The AI agents carried out the following responsibilities:

- **Analyze economic and market trends:** The team trained the AI agent to recognize important key data points, standardize the dataset, and securely store it for data integrity, historical record-keeping, and compliance purposes. Using this curated dataset, the AI agent now evaluates the information to determine the most significant market and economic trends

continued ↘

that have affected, and will likely affect, RIAs and their ability to effectively balance portfolios in the short term.

- **Define and create appropriate themes:** With guidance from the product management team, the AI agents proactively generate investment themes and map them to the highest-performing funds within each theme. For instance, the AI agents could develop themes for:

  - Inflation hedging and currency protection strategies incorporated into liquid ETFs
  - Comparative analysis of asset class performance and decision modeling for portfolio rebalancing
  - Geopolitical risk assessment and scenario planning

- **Create personalized and consistent communication:** The AI agent develops personas for each individual sales prospect (e.g., RIA) by leveraging internal and external data. It then personalizes preapproved email templates for the targeted leads and clients, concentrating on the themes and funds most relevant to each unique prospect.

- **Automate prospect communications, CRM data, and reporting:** AI agents empower knowledge workers to prioritize revenue growth and customer satisfaction by automating tasks. For example:

  - Automate prospect communications, CRM data, and reporting.
  - All outgoing communications are routed to the compliance department for review. Once approved, the AI agent sends the email on behalf of the sales rep. It then monitors responses and routes all communications to the appropriate sales rep for interactive follow-up.
  - The AI agent monitors and analyzes the performance of the overall outreach and individual emails. This data, along with insights gathered during market trend analysis and fund mapping, is integrated into individual RIA profiles. These

profiles are accessible to management, portfolio managers, and marketing teams to guide overall outreach strategies. AI agents update profiles as new information or insights emerge, with manager review and approval options.

- **Facilitate regulatory compliance:** AI agents monitor and audit every action and decision they make in their roles. Compliance teams can easily access and integrate the audit data into their overall corporate reporting obligations. AI agents are programmed to exclusively use preapproved communication templates and information that adheres to regulatory compliance requirements. This eliminates compliance risks from impromptu, noncompliant communications and ensures consistency across all customer and prospect interactions.

Asset management firms must explore innovative approaches to streamline sales processes and attract new clients. By deploying AI agents, this asset manager:

- Accelerated sales growth by identifying high-potential leads and automating personalized outreach

- Increased AUM by equipping fund managers with valuable insights into market trends and customer needs

- Boosted sales team productivity by automating complex manual tasks, allowing reps to dedicate more time to relationship building and deal closing

*Source: Ampliforce*
*Be sure to review the case studies in the Appendix to explore specific quantitative impacts of AI agents.*

The value of AI agents is obvious. Yet, we still must be thoughtful in the way we introduce and deploy them within our organizations to assure optimal success. Next, we'll discuss just how to do that.

# Chapter Takeaways

- AI agents are far more than simple automation. They execute creative and complex tasks. As AI agents learn and work with their human partners, their knowledge expands.

- The first step in deploying an AI agent is to create a job description that clearly defines responsibilities and work it is to accomplish.

- To document the tasks in a workflow, an AI agent observes a knowledge worker at each step, then creates the digital process map.

- Digital process maps serve as an initial and ongoing training system for AI agents to learn their jobs. These maps also document a highly detailed definition of key processes for the organization.

- When a job changes, a knowledge worker simply updates the digital process map and retrains the AI agent, and it is upgraded to the new job requirements.

- AI agents are trained to bring knowledge workers into the loop when they encounter requests that they are unsure how to handle or that require authorization from a manager.

- Organizations and individuals remotely monitor an AI agent's activities in real time, from the worker's own virtual space or via a dashboard.

- As seen in the case study, AI agents do more than automate processes. They intelligently research, analyze, and summarize information, make recommendations, profile targets, and apply their research to personalized content.

# 6

# KEYS TO YOUR SUCCESS

## Chapter Preview

We've discussed how to deploy AI agents themselves. How you ensure your organization's acceptance of AI agents is also critical. Key areas that you need to ask yourself about include:

- How will you view your AI agents? For example, how will you approach organizational charts, hiring plans, and training plans as you expand and shift the roles of knowledge workers?

- How will you introduce your AI agents in a way that creates acceptance? How will you assuage the fear of job replacement and AI concerns?

- How will you fuel collaboration between knowledge workers and AI agents? Between managers and AI agents? Between executives and AI agents?

- What specific organizational programs and approaches are proven to amplify the acceptance of AI agents?

- How do we measure productivity going forward, for both AI agents and their knowledge worker counterparts? Is output really the best measure of knowledge worker productivity?

continued ➘

- What are the keys to successful upskilling and reskilling programs for your human workers? What do these programs look like, and how are they introduced? How do you motivate employees to take advantage of this value?

- How do you identify and mitigate the risks associated with new technology, and specifically AI, going forward?

You now have a fundamental understanding of AI agents: what they are, what they can do, how they do it, and why you need them. You also have answers to the most common questions around deploying AI agents.

Next, let's explore areas you need to address to ensure a successful Digital Workforce.

# IMAGINING YOUR DIGITAL WORKFORCE

Can you imagine your organization of the future, with collaborative teams of digital and human workers fueling productivity, performance, engagement, and innovation?

As we think about this future, we begin to shift the way we think about our workforce.

We will create a new category of worker, an AI agent that is part and parcel of your organizational growth and expansion. They'll be included in organization charts and teaming plans. They'll often be hired to accompany new knowledge workers as we scale and grow.

Just as we create hiring and training plans for our human workforce, we will do the same for our Digital Workforce. New AI agents will be deployed as we learn and discover new and high-value work opportunities for them, just as we hire human workers for new roles.

The good news is that AI agents are easy to manage as part of your workforce. They are a truly dynamic resource that can easily scale and adapt to changing business requirements.

For example, AI agents are

- **Easy to hire and fire.** Since AI agents are software, they can be hired (a.k.a. deployed) and fired (recalled) easily or reskilled.

- **Easy to deploy.** We'll easily create and configure new AI agents with the necessary skills, logic, and technology, then deploy them. No search firms, no interview scheduling shuffles, no HR paperwork.

- **Easy to scale.** When we need more AI agents, we simply specify the job and hire them. Or duplicate AI agents we already have in place.

- **Easy to update and adapt.** As roles and processes change and evolve, AI agents can and will easily adapt and expand with the needs of the organization—immediately.

- **Easy to change focus areas.** Need the same basic worker for a different workflow or data sources? Just update the digital map, train your AI agent, and you have your worker.

## Introducing Your AI Agents

How your knowledge workers accept and use AI agents is critical to their success within your organization. That's why prioritizing the preparation of human workers for the introduction of AI agents is paramount. First, let's address the elephant in the room—the fear, perpetuated by some, that AI will lead to mass job loss as humans are replaced by AI agents. It's not surprising that, according to the report *Work, Workforce, Workers*, over half of workers globally worry about losing jobs to automation.[1] Major technological disruptions, from manufacturing automation to the rise of e-commerce, have historically sparked similar job insecurity. However, research shows that while some worker displacement occurs, it is offset in the long run by the creation of new jobs made possible by the technology. In fact, most long-term employment growth stems from new occupations enabled by innovations. The labor cost savings, job creation effects, and productivity gains from non-displaced workers even raise the prospect of an AI-driven productivity boom that could substantially raise economic growth.[2]

## Fueling Collaboration

It's clear that organizational leaders must remove the mystery behind, and fear of, AI agents for knowledge workers to embrace them. How can you accomplish that?

- Knowledge workers must first understand the strengths and weaknesses of AI agents and share how they are being used and how their deployment serves to further both the organization's objectives and individual workers' success.

- Focus on the high-impact areas where AI agents will contribute. Help employees understand the specifics of their roles and how the AI agents will improve the overall work environment.

- For each individual role, define specific examples of how AI agents will amplify productivity while off-loading the mundane tasks that knowledge workers dislike. Share these specific examples with the corresponding knowledge workers. Be very specific on which tasks the AI agent will assume, delineating the low-value tasks assigned to the AI agent from the high-value work that knowledge workers will continue to perform.

- Continuously stress that AI agents are partners or collaborators for knowledge workers, not replacements for them.

- Create organizational charts that show AI agents as admins or assistants to their knowledge workers. Stress the partnership and collaboration aspect, and that AI agents are designed to help the knowledge workers do the jobs they want to do.

However, encouraging individual partnerships is not enough. To fully realize AI's potential, a cross-organizational approach is key. As the *Harvard Business Review* article "Building the AI-Powered Organization" notes, siloed AI implementations inhibit broad adoption.[3] The biggest impact comes when workflows and processes are holistically realigned and optimized across the enterprise to leverage AI.

This approach not only considers AI opportunities across operational silos but also involves a wide range of human workers in the AI agent rollout, driving broader adoption, which enables the AI agents and their AI technology to have the most significant results when workflows and processes are realigned and optimized across the organization, versus in tactical silos, as with basic automation.[4]

By leveraging a cross-organizational approach to AI agent adoption, teams can review the complete scale of operational flows that can be amplified by AI agents across silos of the organization. This approach also involves a number of human workers across the organization in the adoption of AI agents, fueling broader adoption.

## Amplifying AI Agent Acceptance

It's critical that your entire organization has experience with AI agents to eliminate fear and create excitement and acceptance.

Following are ideas to further amplify AI agents with your employees and managers.

- **Deploy pilot AI agents with key employee influencers.**
  - Be sure these influencers fully understand what an AI agent is, what it is designed to do, and how it supports and amplifies the work of human workers.
  - Then, partner AI agents with these influencers. Give them the support they need to demonstrate that the AI agents are, indeed, off-loading dreaded "busy work" and enhancing the knowledge workers' overall experience and their ability to perform.
  - Ask the influencers to share their experiences, and their excitement, with others in your organization.

- **Include management in your early discussions about AI agents, ahead of, or with, your pilot employees.**
  - Since managers will be overseeing both human and AI agents, it's important they have the knowledge, tools, and information they need to support all their employees' success.
  - As productivity shifts and increases, so will the pace of work. We need to prepare our managers to handle the new accelerated processes and outputs.

- Managers should deploy their own AI agents to support their management role. AI agents can prepare reports, analyze productivity outputs and outcomes, and provide detailed insights managers need to empower their teams.

- **Deploy AI agents to better engage with your human workforce. This enables human workers to interact with their digital counterparts in ways that support the employees beyond the job.**

  - Deploy an AI agent to answer employee questions about the company, its goals, its market position, its products, and other popular questions. This worker can even answer questions about itself and other AI agents. So often, employees feel out of the loop about their company. AI agents can fill this gap, sharing interesting and relevant company information with employees. You'll have better-informed employees, as they experience an AI agent's value in a nonthreatening way.

  - AI agents can handle employee HR requests about everything from payroll disbursements to insurance coverage. Employees can ask questions or request instruction, and the AI agent will quickly fulfill their request.

  - Use AI agents for scheduling meetings. Use AI agents across the organization to off-load the calendaring function for employees. The time savings and decreased frustration will offer everyone the chance to experience the value of an AI agent.

  - Use AI agents as trainers for new employees or new roles. AI agents make great teachers for new employees, for updating information for current employees, and for a wide range of corporate governance training. As you use them to engage with employees, you'll also be able to gather feedback on their interactions to tune and improve the training.

## Measuring What Matters

Traditionally, we have measured productivity based on the increase in output over input.

Outputs are most often associated with increasing productivity through cost cutting. They are a holdover from historical productivity measures in sectors including manufacturing and agriculture.

When measuring the productivity of a factory worker, it's relatively easy to look at the number of parts (outputs) produced for a given unit of labor (inputs).

The productivity of laborers, blue-collar workers, and administrative white-collar workers can be increased simply by lowering costs, consolidating their responsibilities, or eliminating their positions through basic automation. It's a mathematical approach to productivity increases; you increase output by decreasing the cost of inputs.

Look at robots in manufacturing or ATMs in banking. Productivity is easily increased in these cases because these jobs are primarily cost driven. The lower the cost, the higher the productivity.

The output approach to measurement works well when tasks are highly structured and require little if any orchestration. An ATM demonstrates automation at its most basic level; there's no variation in what it does, no skills to be learned or new patterns to be discovered in how it performs work. It's simply a lower cost and more accurate alternative to a human.

Knowledge Work, on the other hand, is value driven. The ultimate objective is to innovate and increase value. This is why I believe the best measurement for knowledge workers' performance is based on outcomes.

# Outputs vs. Outcomes

In a world where AI agents perform repetitive, time-consuming tasks—empowering knowledge workers to focus on high-value work—we will reimagine work and current evaluation metrics. As AI agents assume productivity outputs, knowledge workers will be measured on the value of their work. While outputs are the best measure for AI agents, outcomes are the best measure for knowledge workers.

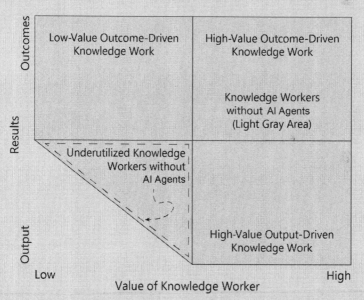

**Figure 6.1** Traditional Knowledge Worker Roles
Source: Ampliforce

As you can see in Figure 6.1, without AI agents, knowledge workers must perform a variety of low-value, output-driven work.

continued ⬊

This is a poor use of their time. It also results in numerous errors since the tasks involved in the lower-left quadrant are tedious and repetitive, *and* it leads to burnout and reduced employee satisfaction.

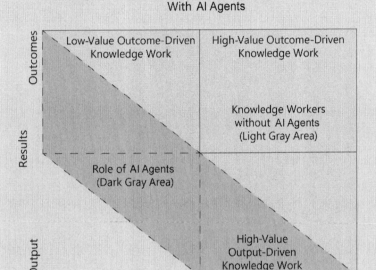

Figure 6.2 Moving Knowledge Workers from Output to Outcome
Source: Ampliforce

In Figure 6.2, we see how AI agents can off-load the burden of tasks in the lower-left quadrant *while increasing the accuracy of this work.*

The bigger benefit is the resulting increase in the time knowledge workers spend in high-value, outcome-based work.

For example, an HR director's productivity could easily be measured by

- The number of candidates searched

- The number of interviews conducted

- How many offer letters were sent out

None of these measures are indicative of how well suited new employees are to their positions, or how successful they will be at fulfilling their responsibilities. Instead, it's measuring value based on volume alone.

If you explore outcome-driven measurements, the HR director's goal would be to hire quality candidates who are an asset to the organization.

In this example, AI agents maximize tactical outputs (the volume metrics of output), increasing the high-value time the HR director spends delivering superior candidates (the outcome).

As you can see, applying traditional output measures to Knowledge Work creates challenges. As we employ AI agents, we can truly measure what matters.

That's a key distinction to make.

It's time to shift our thinking—distinguishing between an output and an outcome—to fully measure and manage productivity in the coming world of AI agents and human workers.

## UPSKILLING AND RESKILLING YOUR ORGANIZATION

We've come to expect that new technology will change the nature of work. Yet the advanced technologies of GenAI, machine learning, and more will accelerate the pace of change beyond anything we've experienced.

We've all heard the doomsayers' claims: "AI will replace human workers. The end is near for employment as robots and software workers take over the world."

While some roles have been automated in select industries, we've simultaneously experienced the creation of new roles *thanks to this automation.*

This is where upskilling and reskilling come into play. First, let's note the difference in goals between the two.

**Upskilling** helps an employee continue to perform in a role that has changed or expanded. Upskilling enhances an employee's existing abilities by teaching them new skills or more advanced skills. There are many cases when an updated position requires additional expertise, which is available thanks to upskilling.

**Reskilling** provides current workers with the skills and knowledge they need for a new and different role. Their position may no longer be needed, the role may have been up leveled to a new role, or there may be an entirely new position that the current worker is going to fill. Instead of losing workers due to changes, the company trains these workers to fulfill new roles in a newly defined career path.

## An Upskilling Example

Upskilling current employees is far more preferable to losing them, given the high costs of employee turnover and training new hires from scratch. This is especially true in today's tight labor market.[5]

While many believe pay is the main reason people leave jobs, research shows that a lack of career growth and development opportunities is actually one of the biggest drivers of turnover, regardless of industry. A Global Talent Monitor survey found 40 percent of departing employees were dissatisfied with the lack of future career development at their company.[6]

Knowledge workers in particular don't want to feel stuck in an unchallenging, boring role. They crave interesting work, opportunities to learn new skills, and a sense that their company has a plan to advance their career over time.[7]

Consider the example of upskilling a data-entry worker whose job is transforming as the company introduces AI to automate repetitive tasks:

- First, the manager clearly explains to the employee why upskilling is being offered, what training and support the company will provide, and how it will empower them to succeed in their adapted role as AI is integrated.[8]

- Next, the specific skills gaps between the worker's current abilities and those needed for the upgraded role are identified. A personalized upskilling plan is developed and documented with the employee, along with future career path opportunities.[9]

- The worker then receives access to a tailored upskilling program, which could include online courses, tuition reimbursement for outside classes, job shadowing, hands-on practice with new tools, and other blended learning methods based on their needs.[10]

- Upon completing the upskilling, the employee transitions into their transformed role, with ongoing support, coaching, and additional training available to set them up for long-term success.[11]

The keys are proactive communication, collaborative planning with everyone, and providing practical learning experiences that impart the necessary skills for employees to thrive as AI reshapes their jobs. Companies that invest in upskilling in this way can boost retention while ensuring their workforce keeps pace in the age of AI.[12]

# A Reskilling Example

We reskill an employee when we train them on an entirely new role. Perhaps it's working with a new technology we've recently deployed, or when we add to their skill sets as we enter a new market or deliver a new product.

For the purposes of our discussion, let's note that reskilling will often result from AI agents uncovering new, expanded roles for knowledge workers.

Let's take a simple example. We all know how much time we spend researching competitors, opportunities, customers and prospects, market trends, and relevant industry happenings on the internet.

Now, imagine you're a researcher in the financial services industry. A new AI agent is performing your research, returning it to you for inputs, and then continuing research based on your preferences. You now receive the research you need, without spending the volume of hours parsing through your internet search overloads.

You now have hours, if not days, of time that you can spend performing more in-depth and detailed analysis of this information. You can also ask your AI agent to search for specific details you discover you'd like to have, as you work through your analysis.

Your role has shifted to a clear focus on using your intelligence, creativity, and skills to deliver higher-value analysis and reporting. As part of this shift, your role now requires deep analysis, especially when it comes to more advanced computational analytics.

You'll need new training to perform this very different role.

This is an example of an *upskilling opportunity created by AI agents as they off-load mundane and time-intensive tasks from human workers.*

By *reskilling* current workers to perform new functions, we create higher-level roles and better engagement with our workforce.

## Reskilling or Upskilling Programs

While many view AI as a job killer or "worker replacement strategy," moving to adopt the technology while leaving the current organization, its processes, and its roles unchanged is a mistake. That's not the best way to apply these advanced technologies, nor is it the most effective workforce management approach.

When we view AI and AI agents as an opportunity to reimagine our world, we create the mindset to understand and capture how these technologies can and will create new processes, new opportunities for revenue and cost savings, and new roles.

We can and will reimagine work, and our organizations, as we onboard these exciting new technologies that will amplify our workforce potential in so many ways. Simultaneously, we can show our workers that we are committed to them, to their career paths, and to preparing them for new opportunities.

## Enticing Employees to Train

How can you entice employees to accept your upskilling or reskilling offers? Following are key actions and approaches for leaders to explore.

- Recognize that change is scary for many, especially when it impacts personal lives and incomes. The more specifics you can share, and the more understanding you are of the fear surrounding the potential changes, the better you'll be able to communicate with and assure employees.

- Be sure to share your vision of how AI agents will strategically benefit your organization, your managers, and your individual

continued ↘

employees. Articulating the whys behind AI agents as they relate to your business planning and goals helps employees better understand the reason behind the shifts.

- Share the rewards your employees will receive thanks to participating in a reskilling or upskilling program. This includes what skills they will develop, how this fulfills their overarching career paths, and why this training is relevant to their career path within the organization.

- Each employee should understand their career path, how AI agents can enhance and even accelerate it, and how the program gives them even broader opportunities in your organization, and even the market at large.

- Keep an eye on how your organization will continue to change in the future. Be sure your employees understand how what they are learning supports the strategic direction of the business. Also, be sure your programs include skills that you have identified as key to your future business.

- Learning new skills as an adult isn't typically a high priority. Employees often feel isolated and demoralized when asked to further their training. Cohort training has been traditionally applied in formal education settings, yet it offers value in reskilling and upskilling scenarios. Training with fellow workers helps individuals feel that they aren't alone, as they share the experiences of learning to help each other succeed.

- Include managers and executives in training programs. These roles share a need to understand how to best use and apply new technologies to their roles. For example, executives can learn how best to use Generative AI as well as understand how to avoid the risks associated with its use, today and in the future.

It's critical that all programs demonstrate that your organization is committed to your employees and the career path that optimizes their skills, expertise, intelligence, and potential.

As part of this, be sure your workers understand that, while AI agents can assume more complex tasks, by off-loading knowledge workers, they are enabling new and more exciting opportunities that we haven't even discovered yet. As your organization shifts, the opportunity to amplify individual career paths toward a higher-value future is part and parcel of every single shift.

## Reskilling/Upskilling Fuels Employee Retention

In today's competitive business landscape, forward-thinking companies recognize that a comprehensive employee value proposition is essential for attracting and retaining top talent. Rather than simply reacting to the demands of the moment, such as signing bonuses or remote work arrangements, these organizations are taking a holistic, systemic approach to engaging and supporting their workforce.[13]

A well-designed employee value proposition goes beyond material offerings and focuses on four key factors: opportunities for growth and development, a sense of connection and community, alignment with the company's meaning and purpose, and competitive compensation and benefits. By integrating these elements into a cohesive system, companies can create an environment that enables employees to reach their full potential and thrive over the long term.[14]

An example of this approach in action is McDonald's Archways to Opportunity program, which includes a mobile application called Archways to Careers. This innovative app helps McDonald's restaurant employees identify and leverage the valuable skills they develop while working at the company. It provides users with tools to explore various career paths, both within McDonald's and in other industries, by mapping their acquired skills to potential future roles. Through this platform, employees can access resources for upskilling and

continued ↘

reskilling, including tuition assistance, career advisors, and local education opportunities, supporting their long-term career development aspirations.

By offering comprehensive training and development programs as part of their employee value proposition, companies like McDonald's demonstrate a commitment to their employees' growth and success. This not only helps attract and retain top talent but also fosters a culture of continuous learning and improvement that benefits both individuals and the organization as a whole.[15]

As the business landscape continues to evolve, companies that take a systemic approach to their employee value proposition will be best positioned to adapt and thrive. By continually assessing employees' needs, engaging in open communication, and updating their offerings accordingly, these organizations can create a compelling narrative that resonates with both current and prospective staff members, setting themselves apart in the competition for talent.

Finally, it's critical to address the resistance you may feel from managers as you introduce training programs. It's only natural. Reskilling or upskilling takes employees away from their job, impacting work productivity and outcomes. It's also a threat to managers who wish to retain their talent, as workers uplevel skills and apply for different roles in the organization. Managers need to understand that you understand their concern and that it is your intent to optimize their organizations, and them, for success.

# MANAGING RISK

As we've deployed more diverse technology, we've introduced more risk in how we protect and manage critical corporate and personal information.

We've all seen the results of security breaches: news and social media blasting company names and the details of the breaches, customers leaving for safer alternatives, not to mention the vast amounts of time and money spent on crisis management as we attempt damage control.

We all know now that the way we manage and protect data has a significant impact on our brand, our employees, our customers and partners, and our bottom line.

The advent of Generative AI escalates this risk. We've all heard the stories of Generative AI's tendency to "hallucinate" or deliver fairy tale responses. We are also experiencing definitive responses that are just plain false. Then there's the issue of leveraging data from the Generative AI system that is, in fact, private and confidential information.

The risks continue to multiply. The burden of managing these risks, from information accuracy to copyrights and individual privacy, is already becoming significant.

Part of the challenge, as we've discussed, is the lack of transparency from Generative AI. You receive a response, but have no knowledge of the underlying information, the logic used to create the response, or the decision logic behind that specific response.

This lack of transparency makes it impossible to monitor Generative AI. Your organization is blind to potential copyright violations, security violations, information inaccuracies, and compliance violations.

As you now know, AI agents provide a comprehensive audit trail of their actions, the data accessed, and the logic applied to specific processes and outcomes.

Consequently, AI agents reduce the risks associated with leveraging Generative AI as part of complex workflows that involve diverse data sources, logic-based decisions, and, especially, internet-based information.

AI agents can also be deployed to identify potential risks, whether within internal organizational processes or due to external threats.

We've explored the capabilities of AI agents, the Amplification Effect they deliver, and the best-practice approaches to introducing and deploying them into your organization.

Next, we'll close with some final thoughts on the Future of Work with our hybrid workforce.

*If you'd like to reimagine work in the not-so-distant future, where AI agents and human workers collaborate to drive innovative business growth, check out the case studies in the Appendix.*

## Chapter Takeaways

As we imagine our organization of the future, we must shift the way we think about our workforce.

The first step is to start thinking of AI agents as a part of our overall workforce, with their own unique needs and measurements. They'll be included in organizational charts, team planning, and hiring and training exercises.

Your organization must address the elephant in the room, a.k.a. the doomsdayers spreading the fear of AI replacing human workers. We must remove the mystery around AI agents. Offer opportunities for all employees to experience their value: train your employees on how they work, what they do, and how the AI agent is dependent on human workers for direction, approvals, problem-solving, and many decisions.

Traditional measurements of output as the productivity metric are applicable for AI agents. As tactical output tasks are off-loaded to AI agents, knowledge workers are best measured by their performance outcomes going forward.

AI agents will drive new roles as part of increased innovation. Organizations must be prepared with reskilling and upskilling programs for knowledge workers to expand their skills in the organization.

AI and other advanced technologies introduce risk around accuracy, privacy, IP protection, and more. AI agents reduce these risks by intelligently automating the comprehensive monitoring and auditing of every action taken. AI agents can monitor, identify, and respond to risk, including alerting the appropriate human workers.

# EPILOGUE:
# REIMAGINING THE FUTURE OF WORK

By now you understand . . .

The adoption of AI agents is not optional, it's inevitable. You have the opportunity to be at the forefront of the AI Agent Mandate, reimagining work to increase revenues, decrease costs, mitigate risks, and leverage information in ways you've never dreamed possible before.

The future of work is already being transformed. The rise of simple chatbots and digital assistants was merely an initial step forward. AI agents and advances in technology will dramatically change the way we work, create value, and build a future for our organizations and our workforces.

We either step up to embrace this opportunity, or we fall behind.

## THE RATHER LARGE ELEPHANT IN THE ROOM

We all hear the caustic claims about the impact of artificial intelligence, and therefore AI agents, on our human workforces.

With so much media coverage flaming the fear of the worst-case scenarios, people are truly afraid of AI taking their jobs. Even Elon Musk, a large promoter of AI, recently stated that he believes that artificial intelligence could eventually put everyone out of a job.[1]

I don't believe that. Rather, our vision at Ampliforce is to *reimagine how work is done* to empower knowledge workers with work that is exciting, creative, and significantly contributes to the success of the business. Our vision is a reconfiguration of the workforce or a reimagined one, one that assigns the manual processes to the AI agents and the critical thinking processes to the knowledge workers. When implemented correctly, this will lead to the empowerment and amplification of humans to achieve their potential, while AI agents will drive increased productivity. Our customers agree and are already experiencing the benefits.

I personally don't believe that AI will take over all work and that humans will be cast out. Do I believe that AI will have the most profound impact on our society over any other technology? Absolutely. Ultimately, I predict that, over time, the most progressive companies will have 20 percent human workers (leadership, customer relationship, quality/compliance controls over AI agents) and 80 percent AI agents.

I will leave you with a final thought . . .

Imagine the opportunity to create an organization where

- Your human workers are fulfilled with creative, thoughtful, and innovative work that fuels their souls, fueling industry-leading employee satisfaction and retention rates.

- Tactical operational work is performed quickly and accurately by your AI agents, leading to optimum productivity levels and outperforming key operational KPIs.

- Your company's amplified execution across all functions leads to a sustained competitive advantage, record bottom-line profits, and maximized shareholder value.

Who wouldn't jump at that chance? There's only one thing standing between you and this outcome for your organization . . .

Hiring your first AI agent.

# APPENDIX 1:
# GLOBAL BANKING AND AI AGENTS

## A CASE STUDY ON DIGITAL WORKFORCE IN ACTION

Let's take a look at a financial services company that Ampliforce worked with to address challenges related to a workforce overloaded with mundane tasks—challenges that any global financial services operation commonly faces. Such tasks were repetitive, time consuming, and error prone, leading to employee burnout, decreased morale, and increased costs.

More importantly, this overload prevented employees from focusing on more strategic and value-added activities that are critical to growth. This hampered bottom-line growth across the diverse divisions, including Markets and Trading, Corporate Banking, and Asset Management of the bank.

More specifically, they were experiencing overloaded business analysts and knowledge workers who were struggling with the analysis of all the complex data they needed to make informed decisions. For example:

- The volume and heterogeneity of the information, plus the speed at which clients and markets generated new data, made it extremely difficult to keep up with analysis and reporting. Key information was often unstructured, semi-structured, and spread across multiple systems, making it difficult and extremely time consuming to consolidate, normalize, and analyze. By the time the data was prepared, it was already out of date.

- The business analysts needed a way to capture real-time insights to make rapid yet informed decisions. Aside from the overwhelming volume of data, they'd found that traditional data-analysis methods were too often time consuming, requiring complex manual computations. This, too, meant that analysis was outdated and potentially irrelevant.

- Business analysts were not successfully identifying the key hidden patterns and trends within the data itself. Identifying these patterns is critical for a variety of banking needs, from understanding corporate health to predicting potential risks to identifying new business opportunities. Using traditional analysis methods, analysts were struggling to compute large calculations needed to identify these subtle yet advantage-driving nuances.

- These issues were prevalent across the bank, from credit risk assessments and fraud detection to valuations and due diligence, to investment and trading recommendations.

## The AI Agent Opportunity

The bank's leadership wanted to explore how AI agents, armed with artificial intelligence (AI), could potentially address these challenges.

The team researched information on the value AI agents bring to the overall organization. They focused on key areas where they felt the agents could best amplify the bank's workforce productivity and overall performance, including

- Leveraging AI agents to orchestrate a wide range of tasks across the organization. Such tasks could include everything from document processing and data entry to market research and reporting to data collection, error correction, consolidation, and analysis. The goal was to free up employees to focus more time on strategic and high-value work, such as developing new products and services, improving customer relationships, and identifying new growth opportunities.

- Improving the efficiency and accuracy of existing processes, from identifying and correcting data errors to offering recommendations for combing or streamlining processes for more efficiency.

- Amplifying the value of knowledge workers by providing real-time insights and recommendations as well as complex analysis of market trends and opportunities, analyzing prospect and customer behavior, accelerating research and reporting, and creating draft content. These time-consuming tasks were critical to the bank's success, yet they caused so much distraction that analysts often had little time to fully review and focus on the information they collected.

- Identifying and mitigating risk associated with regulatory compliance, including identifying and proactively preventing violations, actively tracking and auditing all compliance operations, and ultimately intelligently automating the entire process.

The team noted significant improvement in many areas; the amount of improvement correlated with the degree of automation readiness. They learned that the typical amplification experienced by financial services customers with AI agents included

- **Reduction in manual tasks,** which measured in range from 20 to 80 percent, freeing knowledge workers to focus on high-value work.

- **Error elimination.** AI agents eliminated 80–90 percent of errors in data entry, consolidation, and reporting in their initial work. Data quality was improved by up to 70 percent, with further increases expected as the AI agents learned their jobs and optimized their work.

- **Reduced processing time.** Overall processing time was reduced by 50–90 percent. For example, trade order routing, confirmations, and settlements processing times were reduced by up to 70 percent.

- **Reduced costs.** Overall, workforce costs were reduced by 15–40 percent as AI agents assumed the jobs of orchestrating complex yet highly repetitive workflows.

The team agreed on the key work that would deliver the highest value to the organization and its knowledge workers, focusing on complex operational work, data analysis, market research, and compliance. These processes were critical to the bank but also extremely time consuming.

Each division identified candidate processes that fell into the complex operational category, and the AI agents were hired.

Following are the individual cases of AI agents for each bank division.

# CORPORATE BANKING AND AI AGENTS

Corporate banking provides a range of financial services to large corporate clients, including cash management, trade finance, portfolio management, and lending.

Business analysts were struggling to deliver the real-time insights and recommendations corporate clients expect, given the volume, speed, and heterogeneity of the data that fueled these analyses.

The division's leaders decided to focus their AI agents first on work that would free the business analysts from the high volume of data collection, normalization, and consolidation, as well as analytics and reporting.

## Before AI Agents

Corporate banking relies heavily on analyses of rich, diverse data concerning individual corporate clients and their market positions, from financial statements, market data, and credit history to market trends, company fundamentals, competitor data, and customer transaction patterns. The information used for analysis and recommendations is located across a variety of internal and external sources to the bank and the corporate client. Before AI agents, here are some of the ways corporate bankers used their time:

- Corporate business analysts spent volumes of time finding, collecting, and consolidating data from these heterogeneous sources.

- They also spent an inordinate amount of time correcting and normalizing this disparate data. For example, data varies in format and convention between various applications. When diverse data is consolidated for analysis, these differences must be normalized. Errors and inconsistencies must also be identified and corrected. As data grows and diversity accelerates, normalization requires more and more manual effort from analysts.

- Many created spreadsheets to consolidate and review the data, manually entering the data fields as they moved from application to application.

- There was significant work required to document the tedious details to support the bank's regulatory compliance. The analysts were also working to proactively predict or detect regulatory issues in advance but had not found an effective method.

AI agents were created and deployed for the Corporate Banking division to solve these problems.

## After AI Agents

AI agents were deployed to support business analysts in areas including credit risk assessment, fraud detection, investment banking, and regulatory compliance.

The AI agents observed business analysts in their roles and created digital maps for training. Once trained, they began their duties, collaborating with their business analyst partners.

To zero in on one particular area, this explanation focuses on the impact of AI agents on the credit risk assessment process for corporate banking.

**Credit Risk Assessment**

Credit risk assessment is performed by credit analysts who are experienced in analyzing and critically reviewing a corporation's financial standing.

AI agents were deployed to support the credit analysts in their work. Today, AI agents perform key work in support of their analyst partners, by doing the following:

- **Knowing your customer.** AI agents gather and cross-check all the relevant information about the borrower, including name, address, income, assets, liabilities, credit history, employment history, any record of fraud, and any other relevant information that impacts the loan. AI agents collect insights from the internet, social media, and more. This information is given to the credit analysts for their analysis and review.

- **Collecting information on potential nonfinancial risks.** AI agents research and collect key information concerning nonfinancial risks, such as geopolitical, regulatory, reputational, operational, and compliance risks. The information is collected, consolidated, normalized, and cross-checked, then shared with the credit analysts.

- **Analyzing information.** After collecting and normalizing the data, AI agents analyze the borrower's financial data, including their balance sheet, income statement, and cash flow statement. They also collect background information for a corporate audit for their human partners to review, as well as provide a preliminary analysis on cash flow drivers and projections.

- **Understanding the business.** Since credit analysts need to understand the business beyond financial data, AI agents also collect information on the business itself, including the borrower's industry, market position, competitive landscape, and social status. This information is consolidated, then shared with analysts.

- **Recommending loan pricing.** Many complex factors determine the final rate offered by the bank, beyond the borrower's specific factors. AI agents now collect key insights, including interest rates, moratorium periods, floating (primarily loan pricings are based on this), and money movement rates. Comparison information and analysis are also provided to the credit analysts so that they can make the best and most consistent loan pricing decisions.

The credit analysts were a bit apprehensive of the AI agents when they were first hired, but they quickly appreciated the value derived from these 24/7 workers, such as:

- The AI agents provide the credit analysts with more data than they usually identified themselves, delivered in a fully normalized and ready-to-analyze form. Additionally, the analysts can focus on creating highly accurate and well-informed insights and recommendations.

- Since the AI agents can spend time enlarging the data pool using social media data, internet information, media articles, and third-party reports, analysts are now able to create a more refined picture of a borrower's financial situation. They can now provide additional insights to help the bank make more accurate predictions about the corporation's ability to repay a loan.

- The credit analysts learned that the recommendations from the AI agent were well thought out and actionable. They now rely on them to do the first wave of analysis of information, providing a baseline for the credit analysts to review. Analysts can also dive deeper into specific data as needed, focusing on critical areas that require additional scrutiny.

- The analysts also benefit from being able to ask the AI agents to find specific information that is lacking or seems out of line with expectations. AI agents quickly supplement critical new data for the analysts to make better, faster recommendations.

## The Amplification Effect

The Amplification Effect, internally referred to as "the Amp Effect," is a powerful concept that encompasses the myriad benefits and value created for customers through the implementation of AI agents. At Ampliforce, we use a customer-centric methodology when addressing our clients' pain points, which was adapted after my time at EMC, using the approach they used to offer solutions to their customers. This methodology focuses on delivering significant improvements in operations, accuracy, consistency, and risk management across various industries and business functions.

One of the key aspects of the Amplification Effect is its ability to drive top-line revenue generation. By providing employees with deeper and more insightful information, AI agents enable them to spend more time analyzing critical business factors and making informed decisions. This leads to the identification of better and more high-value opportunities for the company, as well as the ability to consistently set competitive prices that increase revenues.

In addition to revenue generation, the Amplification Effect also contributes to cost reduction. Prior to the introduction of

AI agents, employees often spent a significant amount of time on research and manual data manipulation—hidden costs that are not readily apparent to the organization. By offloading these time-consuming tasks to AI agents, employees can now focus on work that directly contributes to the bottom line, as well as on developing creative and innovative ways to improve overall business processes. This optimization reduces the time to decision and increases the effectiveness of those decisions, ultimately reducing overhead costs and minimizing errors.

Another critical aspect of the Amplification Effect is its impact on risk mitigation and compliance. AI agents provide a comprehensive audit trail, reducing the costs and effort associated with delivering the audit information required for regulatory compliance. This is a significant improvement over manual data collection from diverse sources or reliance on compliance systems that require careful audit reviews for missing or incorrect data. The resulting audits are of far superior quality, while the effort required is substantially reduced.

In today's global business landscape, the Amplification Effect is particularly relevant due to increased geopolitical risks associated with outsourcing outside of the United States. By leveraging AI agents, companies can maintain control over their processes and data, mitigating the risks inherent in relying on offshore resources. This added benefit further underscores the value of the Amplification Effect in driving business success and resilience in an increasingly complex and uncertain world. The Corporate Banking division received deep and broad value from their first AI agent deployment. Specifically, the Amplification Effect created impacts including:

- **Increase in the optimum high-value loans for the bank.** The AI agents rapidly provide deeper and more insightful information to the credit analysts for review. That means the analysts are able to spend more time analyzing the applicant's overall position and ability to repay the loan, resulting in selecting better and more high-value loan opportunities for the bank. They are also better able to consistently set loan rates to increase bank revenues while remaining competitive in the market.

- **Reduction in the associated costs of loans.** The time spent by credit analysts on research and manual data manipulation were hidden costs to the bank. These became apparent as the AI agents off-loaded these time-consuming tasks from the analysts. Analysts now spend time on work that directly contributes to the bottom line of the bank, as well as on creative and innovative ways to improve the bank's credit assessment and overall loan processes. The result is a highly optimized process that reduces the time to decision and the effectiveness of the loan decision. Consequently, the overhead cost per loan is reduced, as are the number of default loans, both of which significantly reduce the average cost per loan.

- **Risk mitigation and compliance.** The bank enjoys reduced costs and effort associated with delivering the audit information required for regulatory compliance. Instead of manually collecting information from diverse sources or using a compliance system that requires careful audit reviews for missing or incorrect data, the AI agents provide a comprehensive audit trail. The quality of the audits is far superior, while effort is reduced.

- **Quantitative impacts.** Initial impacts of the AI agents measured by the Credit Risk Assessment team across a variety of diverse assessments are shown in the following table.

| Measurement | Amp Effect |
|---|---|
| Reduced assessment time | 50–70% |
| Enhanced accuracy and consistency | 80–95% |
| Improved risk management | 30–45% |
| Fraud detection | 60–80% |
| Regulatory compliance | 40–60% |

Source: Ampliforce

Hiring AI agents to support knowledge workers in credit risk assessments provides substantial improvements in efficiency, accuracy, risk management, and regulatory compliance, contributing to a more profitable and sustainable business. By integrating these sources, the case study accurately reflects the quantitative impacts and benefits of using AI in credit risk assessment.

# INVESTMENT BANKING AND AI AGENTS

Investment banking plays a crucial role in facilitating financial transactions and advising corporations on strategic decisions regarding their investment strategies and tactics.

The division's leaders decided to first focus their AI agents on work that would support investment analysts in delivering more accurate, timely, and innovative investment recommendations.

### Before AI Agents

Within the bank's Investment Banking division, investment banking analysts played a crucial role, providing essential support to senior bankers in financial transactions. However, their productivity was severely hindered by several challenges:

- **Increasing workload and time pressure.** Investment banking analysts were burdened with a demanding workload and tight deadlines as they juggled multiple projects simultaneously. Projects continued to increase, even as the analysts were overwhelmed with the tactical and operational tasks associated with collecting critical insights to identify optimum investment strategies.

- **Manual, repetitive tasks.** A significant portion of an analyst's time was spent on manual, repetitive tasks such as data collection, formatting, and financial modeling. These tasks were tedious and time consuming, reducing the time available for more strategic and value-added work.

- **Inefficient workflow and collaboration.** Investment banking teams were relying on inefficient communication channels and manual handoffs of tasks. This led to delays and miscommunication, limiting analyst collaboration.

- **Lack of access to real-time data and insights.** All too often, analysts relied on outdated or incomplete data, inhibiting the ability to make informed decisions and provide accurate insights.

AI agents were configured and deployed to solve these challenges for the Investment Banking division.

## After AI Agents

AI agents were introduced to support investment analysts in areas including due diligence and valuation, risk assessment and portfolio management, sentiment analysis and market forecasting, and algorithmic trading. AI agents were also tasked with evaluating, updating, optimizing, and managing the CRM system for all investment banking customers.

An AI agent observed investment analysts in their roles and created specific digital maps for specific work. These maps trained the AI agents, and they began their duties, collaborating with and overseen by their investment analyst partners.

Let's explore the specific impact of AI agents on the due diligence and valuation process, specifically, the tedious yet critical creation of comp books.

## Due Diligence and Valuation

Investment analysts perform due diligence and valuation work. They are experienced in researching, analyzing, and evaluating investments based on comparable market opportunities.

AI agents were deployed to amplify these analysts' outcomes. The initial AI agent project focused on creating comparable company analysis decks including industry and sector peer group analysis, performance and valuation benchmarking, and precedent transactions analysis. Specifically, the AI agents were trained to:

- **Analyze data.** AI agents review the specified data sources, including earnings call releases, data from financial institutions, and public data concerning corporate financial positions, for organizations that resemble the target of the due diligence. Key data points to evaluate include geographic location and asset size.

- **Identify comparable targets**. The AI agent identifies twelve to fifteen comparable targets based on their financial profiles and best matches to the due diligence target organization.

- **Generate reports**. After the comparable targets are identified, the AI agent generates a report detailing each key data point for individual comparable targets.

- **Create recommendations**. Using that report, the AI agent offers insights and recommendations it found during its analysis. This recommendation and the report are shared with investment analysts and other identified parties within the organization.

By leveraging AI agents to automate the process of creating comp books, investment analysts can focus their time and expertise on higher-value activities such as interpreting the results, identifying potential risks and opportunities, and making informed investment decisions. The AI agents help to streamline the due diligence process, improve efficiency, and enhance the quality of the analysis by consistently identifying the most relevant comparable targets and providing comprehensive reports.

## The Amplification Effect

AI agents' impacts on the bank's due diligence workflows included enhanced efficiency, accuracy, and risk management capabilities. Impacts included

- **Reduced processing time.** AI agents streamline the due diligence process by automating tasks such as document gathering, verification, and analysis. Processing time is reduced by up to 80 percent, enabling faster deal completion and improved decision-making cycles.

- **Enhanced accuracy and consistency.** Due diligence is dependent on accurate and comprehensive data. AI agents now collect, normalize, and analyze large amounts of data, including financial statements, legal documents, and industry reports. They then generate more accurate and comprehensive due diligence comp books. This enhances data accuracy, assuring consistent and accurate evaluation of potential investment opportunities.

- **Improved risk assessment.** AI agents quickly identify patterns and anomalies in financial and legal data that not only take human analysts significant time but that they might overlook. The AI agents share their analysis with knowledge workers, who then proactively identify and analyze risks associated with prospective investments.

- **Customized due diligence.** The AI agents are trained to analyze comparable assets based on specific industries, asset classes, or investment strategies. This enables knowledge workers to conduct more focused and relevant due diligence assessments using the custom information.

- **Predictive analytics.** AI agents analyze historical data and current trends to predict the likelihood of successful investments. Knowledge workers now use this information to make better-informed decisions concerning deal opportunities and risk allocation.

- **Regulatory compliance.** Since AI agents create a comprehensive audit trail of all actions, compliance reporting time and effort are dramatically reduced. Additionally, an AI agent performs regulatory compliance checks, assuring adherence to all applicable regulations and standards. This reduces the risk of legal and financial penalties.

- **Quantitative impacts.** The initial impacts of the AI agents measured by the due diligence team are shown in the following table.

| Measurement | The Amp Effect |
|---|---|
| Reduced time to completion | 60–80% |
| Enhanced accuracy and consistency | 85–95% |
| Improved risk management | 25%–40% |
| Customized due diligence | 15%–25% |
| Regulatory compliance | 35%–50% |

Source: Ampliforce

Overall, AI agents contribute substantial improvements in efficiency, accuracy, risk management, and regulatory compliance, empowering analysts to create a more profitable and risk-averse investment portfolio.

# MARKET AND TRADING DIVISION

The bank's Market and Trading division facilitates the trading and executing of financial instruments such as stocks, bonds, and currencies.

The division's leaders decided to focus their AI agents first on workflows where the volumes of data and rapidly changing data points overwhelmed analysts to reduce time spent on accurate and real-time analysis and prediction.

**Before AI Agents**

The organization faced several challenges concerning workforce productivity and effectiveness in the Market and Trading division. These challenges included:

- **Manual data gathering and processing.** Market and Trading analysts spent a significant amount of time manually gathering, cleaning, and preparing data from various sources, such as market feeds, news outlets, and internal systems. This manual effort was time consuming and error prone, leading to delays in decision-making and missed opportunities.

- **Information overload and decision fatigue.** Market and Trading analysts were inundated with constant information from various sources, making it challenging to identify and prioritize relevant insights. This information overload led to decision fatigue, impairing their ability to make sound judgments under pressure.

- **Delayed market response.** Traditional market and trading processes often involve lengthy data analysis, decision-making, and order execution cycles. This delayed responses to market changes, impacting profitability and risk management. The time spent on manual data research and collection in support of decisions often delayed critical decisions, resulting in missed opportunities.

- **Limited real-time insights and predictive analytics.** Understanding market trends and predicting price movements in real time is crucial for successful trading. However, manual processes often need to catch up to the pace of the market, hindering timely decision-making.

- **Inefficient risk management and regulatory compliance.** Market and trading activities involve inherent risks, and

financial institutions must adhere to strict regulatory requirements. However, manual risk-management and compliance
processes could have been more efficient and resource intensive, even with compliance tools in place.

AI agents were configured and deployed for the Market and
Trading teams to solve these challenges.

## After AI Agents

AI agents were introduced to support Market and Trading analysts in areas like high-frequency and algorithmic trading, market
surveillance and fraud detection, risk management, portfolio optimization, sentiment analysis and trend prediction, personalized
trading platforms, and regulatory compliance and reporting.

As usual, an AI agent observed the analysts in their roles and
created specific digital maps for training. Trained AI agents immediately began to collaborate with their analysts.

Following is a discussion around the impact of AI agents as measured by the Sentiment and Trend Analysis team within the Market
and Trading division.

## Sentiment Analysis and Trend Prediction

AI agents were introduced to support sentiment and trend analysts in areas including information research, normalization and
consolidation, and preliminary analysis and recommendations
preparation. AI agents were also trained to proactively collaborate

with analysts for ad hoc, real-time analysis, identifying, collecting, and reporting critical data elements these analysts needed for real-time recommendations.

The AI agents were quickly able to support their analyst partners in a variety of ways, amplifying the results delivered by the Market and Trading division.

- **Automated data collection and preparation.** The AI agents began the work of identifying, collecting, and preparing data for the analysts. This eliminates most of the analysts' mundane manual tasks, freeing their time to focus on in-depth analysis and other higher-value tasks.

- **Objective and consistent analysis.** AI agents perform preliminary data analysis based on the logic rules they are trained to follow. They deliver these reports to the analysts using the data itself. This guidance helps sentiment analysts to review the data more consistently, reducing the risk of human error and bias—consequently, the division benefits from more reliable and actionable insights.

- **Real-time analysis and response.** AI agents process and analyze data in real time, providing analysts with timely updates to previous insights. AI agents also respond quickly to analysts' ad hoc requests for data and analysis of rapidly emerging trends and changing customer behaviors and sentiments.

- **Customized insights and predictive analytics.** AI agents generate granular insights tailored to specific customer segments, product offerings, and market regions. AI agents also follow custom logic for specific predictions, identifying and formulating improved data. This enables analysts to better predict future customer behavior and market trends, amplifying proactive decision-making.

## The Amplification Effect

The impacts of AI agents on the bank's sentiment analysis and trend prediction led to substantial benefits, including:

- **Reduced costs.** AI agents reduce costs by eliminating the onerous hours analysts needed to manually research, identify, collect, and prepare data for analysis. Instead, the analysts now apply their time to in-depth analysis, deeper evaluation, and high-value outcomes.

- **Improved customer satisfaction.** The AI agents help their analysts deliver far-reaching and in-depth customer sentiment analysis and reporting. Consequently, the bank makes far better market and trading recommendations, amplifying customer portfolios and satisfaction.

- **Increased revenue.** Now that the analysts have more in-depth, comprehensive, and accurate insights and data, they spend their time thinking creatively and developing new products and services to capture a broader portfolio of customer business, amplifying revenue.

- **Reduced risk.** Using the insights provided by AI agents, analysts are better able to identify risks and take steps to mitigate them.

- **Quantitative impacts.** AI agents collaborated with the Sentiment Analysis and Market Trends team to improve market and trading recommendations.

| Measurement | The Amp Effect |
|---|---|
| Reduced processing time | 80%–90% |
| Enhanced accuracy and consistency | 85%–95% |
| Improved timeliness of insights | 70%–80% |
| Customized analysis | 20%–30% |
| Predictive analytics | 15%–25% |

Source: Ampliforce

AI agents' predictions helped the bank overcome workforce productivity challenges. The division was able to harness the power of data to amplify competitive edge, customer satisfaction, and the value of informed strategic decisions.

# ASSET MANAGEMENT

Asset Management oversees the investment portfolios of individuals and institutions. However, asset managers often need help in effectively analyzing market trends and making informed investment decisions.

The division's leaders decided to focus their AI agents first on work that would support asset managers and analysts in delivering more accurate, timely, and innovative portfolio management recommendations.

**Before AI Agents**

Within the bank's Asset Management division, asset managers and analysts provided essential support to senior bankers in financial transactions. However, several challenges severely hindered their productivity.

- **Data overload and manual processing.** Asset managers were inundated with vast amounts of data from various sources, including financial statements, market reports, and economic indicators. Manually collecting, consolidating, and normalizing this data was time consuming and error prone. Consequently, analysts spent an inordinate amount of time focused on manual data-management tasks, limiting their focus on analytics to derive actionable insights. This also led to missed opportunities and delayed responses to market changes, impacting profitability and risk management.

- **Lack of real-time analysis and response.** Understanding market trends and customer behavior in real time is crucial for effective asset management. Since analysts had to consolidate data manually from diverse sources, they needed a way to effectively analyze and respond to real-time market shifts or time-critical client requests.

- **Limited customization and personalization.** Owing to the volumes of data that required analysis, traditional asset management approaches often relied on standardized models and strategies to optimize their results across a diverse clientele. This approach did not allow analysts to address the unique needs and preferences of individual investors, limiting the effectiveness of portfolio management and impacting overall customer satisfaction.

- **Inefficient regulatory compliance.** Asset managers faced a complex regulatory landscape, requiring extensive manual effort to ensure compliance. This diverted resources from core investment activities and significantly increased operational costs and compliance risk.

## After AI Agents

AI agents were introduced to support asset managers and analysts in areas including sentiment analysis, technical analysis, risk management, and algorithmic trading.

Let's explore the impact of AI agents measured by the Portfolio Management team within the Asset Management division.

## Portfolio Management

AI agents support asset managers and analysts with work encompassing the selection, weighting, and ongoing management of a diversified mix of assets to achieve specific investment objectives and manage risk.

The introduction of AI agents within the Portfolio Construction and Optimization division led to substantial shifts in the way analysts worked, including

- **Reduced processing time.** AI agents now orchestrate manual tasks such as data collection, aggregation, analysis, and report generation. This frees up portfolio managers and analysts to focus on more strategic activities, such as custom portfolio optimization, for high-value outcomes. It also reduces the overall processing time for portfolio construction and rebalancing.

- **Enhanced accuracy and consistency.** AI agents now analyze vast amounts of data, quickly identifying patterns and relationships that may be missed by human analysts. This leads to more accurate and consistent portfolio construction and optimization, reducing the risk of errors and omissions.

- **Accelerated timeliness of insights.** AI agents provide real-time insights into portfolio performance, risk exposures, and market conditions. As a result, portfolio managers now make informed decisions and adjust portfolios promptly. This helps them capture market opportunities and mitigate potential risks before they materialize.

- **Customized portfolio construction.** AI agents are trained with specific logic for individual portfolios, and now help to develop customized portfolio strategies. Thanks to targeted business logic, these strategies consider the specific characteristics of individual clients, their risk tolerance, investment goals, and financial situations. This provides more personalized and effective portfolio management for each client, increasing outcomes and amplifying customer satisfaction.

- **Predictive portfolio optimization.** AI agents use logic and algorithms to predict future market conditions, asset class performance, and risk profiles. Portfolio managers focus on optimizing portfolios proactively for anticipated market shifts and potential risks. This enhances portfolio resilience and improves long-term returns.

## The Amplification Effect

The impacts of AI agents on the bank's Portfolio Management team led to

- **Reduced processing time.** AI agents automate the manual tasks involved in portfolio construction, rebalancing, and performance analysis. The reduction in processing time enables portfolio managers and analysts to focus on more strategic activities.

- **Enhanced accuracy and consistency.** AI agents analyze vast amounts of data and identify patterns that may be missed by human reviewers, leading to more accurate and consistent portfolio construction and optimization. This reduces the risk of errors and improves risk-adjusted returns.

- **Improved timeliness of insights.** AI agents provide real-time insights into portfolio performance, risk exposures, and market conditions, enabling portfolio managers to make informed decisions and adjust portfolios promptly. For example, portfolio managers now have the time and the real-time data to rebalance a portfolio to take advantage of predicted favorable market conditions or to mitigate potential losses in the event of suspected market downturns. This increases the capture of market opportunities and mitigation of possible risks.

- **Customized portfolio construction.** AI agents use logic to develop recommendations for customized portfolio strategies that align with the specific characteristics of individual clients, such as their risk tolerance, investment goals, and financial situations. This provides more personalized and effective portfolio management for each client.

- **Predictive portfolio optimization.** AI agents predict future market conditions, asset class performance, and risk profiles. Portfolio managers proactively optimize portfolios for anticipated market shifts and potential risks. This enhances portfolio resilience and improves long-term returns.

- **Enhanced risk management.** AI agents continuously monitor portfolio risk exposures, identify potential risks, and suggest mitigation strategies. This enables portfolio managers to proactively manage risk, reduce potential losses, and adhere to regulatory requirements.

- **Improved decision-making.** AI agents assist portfolio managers in making informed risk assessments, evaluating investment opportunities, and prioritizing portfolio adjustments. This leads to better decision-making and enhanced risk-adjusted returns.

- **Quantitative impacts.** The following table shows the initial impacts of the AI agents measured by the Portfolio Management team.

| Measurement | The Amp Effect |
|---|---|
| Reduced processing time | 40%–60% |
| Enhanced accuracy and consistency | 80%–90% |
| Improved timeliness of insights | 30%–50% |
| Customized portfolio construction | 15%–25% |
| Predictive portfolio optimization | 10%–20% |
| Enhanced risk management | 15%–25% |
| Improved decision-making | 15%–25% |

Source: Ampliforce

These improvements significantly amplify the efficiency and effectiveness of portfolio management. The bank now constructs more efficient and risk-aligned portfolios, improving client satisfaction and achieving better long-term investor returns.

# RISK MANAGEMENT

Risk management ensures financial institutions identify, assess, and mitigate potential risks that could impact their financial stability and profitability.

### Before AI Agents

Within the bank's Risk Management division, risk managers and analysts identified, assessed, and managed the financial risks that the firm faced in its operations. These risks can arise from various sources, including market risks, credit risks, operational risks, and liquidity risks. Productivity challenges included

- **Data overload and manual processing.** As with every other banking arena, risk managers were inundated with vast amounts of data from various sources, including financial statements, market reports, regulatory filings, and internal systems. Manually processing and analyzing this data was time consuming and error prone, limiting the risk experts' time and ability to derive actionable insights and manage risk effectively.

- **Information silos and fragmented data.** Risk management often involved siloed data and fragmented information across different departments, such as trading, underwriting, and compliance. This fragmentation reduced the analysts' time and ability to perform comprehensive risk assessment, impeding collaboration among risk professionals.

- **Lack of real-time insights and predictive analytics.** Traditional risk-management processes relied on historical data and delayed reporting, lagging behind the pace of the market. This lack of real-time insights and predictive analytics led to delayed risk identification and losses.

- **Inefficient risk modeling and scenario analysis.** Risk modeling and scenario analysis were crucial for understanding potential risks and developing mitigation strategies. Manual modeling processes were extremely time consuming and often needed to capture all relevant factors and scenarios.

- **Regulatory compliance and reporting burden.** As with other divisions, Risk Management faced stringent regulatory requirements for compliance and reporting. Complying with these requirements was significantly resource intensive, diverting attention and focus from core risk-management activities.

AI agents were quickly configured and deployed to support the analysts and managers.

## After AI Agents

AI agents were introduced to support risk managers and analysts in areas including market risk and stress testing, operational risk assessment, liquidity risk, risk governance, and regulatory compliance risk.

The AI agents were trained and began collaborating with their risk-management partners.

Let's explore the impact of AI agents measured by the Risk Management team, specifically regarding market risk analysis and stress testing.

## Market Risk Analysis and Stress Testing

The AI agent for market risk analysis and stress testing analyzes market data, historical trends, and economic indicators to assess market risks, perform stress tests, and develop risk mitigation strategies. Key work includes

- **Automated data collection, aggregation, and analysis.** AI agents now gather, clean, and analyze data from multiple sources, providing risk managers with a consolidated view of risk exposures and market conditions. This significantly reduces the time and effort required for data preparation and analysis while off-loading all these mundane tasks from analysts.

- **Real-time risk monitoring and insights.** AI agents continuously monitor risk exposures in real time, enabling risk managers to identify potential risks promptly and make informed decisions. AI agents also analyze data streams, identify anomalies, and provide alerts for potential breaches of risk limits.

- **Predictive risk analytics and scenario modeling.** AI agents analyze historical data, market trends, and economic indicators to anticipate potential risks and assess the impact of various scenarios. This empowers risk managers to mitigate risks and prepare for potential market shocks proactively.

- **Automated regulatory compliance and reporting.** AI agents create complete audit trails, automating regulatory compliance tasks such as risk reporting, regulatory change management, and compliance audits. This frees risk managers to focus on strategic risk analysis and improving compliance accuracy.

- **Enhanced decision-making and collaboration.** AI agents assist risk managers in making informed risk assessments, evaluating risk-mitigation strategies, and prioritizing risk-management activities. This facilitates collaboration and knowledge sharing among risk professionals across the organization.

## The Amplification Effect

The impacts of AI agents on the bank's Risk Management team included

- **Reduced processing time.** AI agents automate the manual risk identification, assessment, and reporting tasks. This substantial reduction in processing time frees risk managers to focus on more strategic work to proactively minimize the bank's risk.

- **Enhanced accuracy and consistency.** AI agents analyze vast amounts of data and identify patterns that may need to be noticed by human reviewers. This reduces the risk of errors and improves risk-management effectiveness, leading to more accurate and consistent risk assessments and reporting.

- **Improved timeliness of insights.** AI agents provide real-time insights into risk exposures, market conditions, and emerging risks. Risk managers now proactively identify and address potential risks before they materialize, preventing losses and improving overall performance.

- **Customized risk assessment.** AI agents develop customized risk models that consider the specific characteristics of individual portfolios and investment strategies. This provides more accurate and relevant risk assessments for each portfolio.

- **Predictive risk analytics.** AI agents predict future risk exposures based on historical data, market trends, and other factors. Risk managers better anticipate potential risks and proactively take preventive measures.

- **Enhanced risk-management effectiveness.** AI agents continuously monitor risk exposures, identify potential risks, and suggest mitigation strategies. Risk managers now proactively manage risk, reduce potential losses, and adhere to regulatory requirements.

- **Reduced risk-adjusted costs.** By automating tasks, reducing errors, and improving decision-making, AI agents lead to significant cost savings.

- **Improved regulatory compliance.** AI agents automate regulatory compliance tasks, such as risk reporting, regulatory change management, and compliance audits. This empowers risk managers to focus on strategic risk analysis and improve compliance accuracy, saving time and money and avoiding expensive penalties.

- **The quantitative impacts** from the organization are shown in the following table.

| Measurement | The Amp Effect |
|---|---|
| Reduced processing time | 60%–80% |
| Enhanced accuracy and consistency | 85%–95% |
| Improved timeliness of insights | 70%–80% |
| Customized risk assessment | 25%–35% |
| Predictive risk analytics | 15%–25% |
| Enhanced risk-management effectiveness | 20%–30% |
| Reduced risk-adjusted costs | 15%–25% |
| Improved regulatory compliance | 15%–25% |

Source: Ampliforce

Thanks to the introduction of AI agents, risk-management professionals are significantly improving the efficiency, accuracy, and effectiveness of their risk-management practices. Ultimately, this leads to reduced risk exposure, improved financial performance, and enhanced regulatory compliance.

# OPERATIONS

The Operations division ensures the smooth and efficient functioning of the organization's core processes, including transaction processing, customer service, and regulatory compliance.

## Before AI Agents

Operations is responsible for a wide range of tasks, including analyzing and optimizing operational processes, risk management and compliance, data management and reporting, vendor management, and performance measurement. As with other divisions, workforce productivity was suffering due to a significant amount of time and focus being spent on mundane, lower-value tasks. Key challenges included

- **Repetitive and rule-based tasks.** Many operational tasks involved repetitive and rule-based processes, such as account reconciliations, transaction processing, and customer onboarding. These tasks were tedious and time consuming for employees, leading to fatigue, errors, and reduced productivity.

- **Manual data processing and analysis.** Operations professionals spent a significant amount of time manually gathering, cleaning, and preparing data from various sources, such as internal systems, customer records, and external data providers. This manual effort was time consuming and error prone.

- **Inefficient workflows and siloed systems.** Operational processes often involved multiple departments and systems, leading to inefficiencies and delays. Siloed systems and lack of data integration limited collaboration, increased handoff volume and time, and prolonged time to work completion.

- **Limited real-time insights and exception management.** Traditional operational processes often relied on batch processing and delayed reporting, making it challenging to identify and address exceptions or issues in real time. This led to customer dissatisfaction, operational risks, and missed opportunities for proactive intervention.

- **Regulatory compliance and reporting burden.** Financial institutions faced stringent regulatory requirements for operations processes, such as Know Your Customer (KYC), Anti–Money Laundering (AML), as well as data privacy compliance. Manual compliance tasks were resource intensive and diverted attention from core operational activities, even with compliance tools in place.

AI agents were quickly trained and deployed to support the operational professionals and analysts.

## After AI Agents

AI agents were introduced to support operations in areas including regulatory compliance monitoring and reporting, risk management, vendor management, and performance measurement.

Once trained, they began their duties, working with their operational partners.

Following are key impacts created by AI agents, as measured by the Operations team, specifically around regulatory compliance monitoring and reporting.

## Regulatory Compliance Monitoring and Reporting

The AI agent for regulatory compliance focuses on risk assessments, orchestrating compliance monitoring, generating compliance reports, maintaining compliance records, and continuously improving compliance processes.

AI agents bring an innate advantage to compliance work. Since AI agents automatically create a complete audit trail of all actions, they provide detailed compliance-reporting information as they work.

The compliance AI agent first optimizes the compliance recording and reporting workflow to include the data from other AI agents. The AI agent now contributes to the effectiveness of compliance monitoring and reporting in a variety of aspects.

- **Automated data aggregation and analysis.** AI agents efficiently gather, clean, and analyze data from multiple sources, providing operations professionals with a consolidated view of operational data. This significantly reduces the time and effort required for data preparation and analysis.

- **Automated regulatory compliance and reporting.** AI agents automate regulatory compliance tasks, including data aggregation, reporting, and risk assessment. This off-loads compliance officers to focus on strategic risk analysis and reduces the risk of regulatory violations.

- **Off-loading repetitive tasks.** AI agents now automate repetitive and rule-based tasks, such as account reconciliations, transaction processing, and customer onboarding. This frees significant employee time to focus on more complex issues.

- **Workflow optimization and process integration.** AI agents analyze operational workflows, identify bottlenecks, and suggest improvements for streamlining processes and reducing hand-offs. AI agents also facilitate data integration between systems, enabling seamless communication and collaboration across departments.

- **Real-time analytics and exception management.** AI agents are trained in the necessary logic to continuously monitor operational data, identify anomalies, and alert operations professionals to potential issues or exceptions in real time. AI agents also perform human error modeling, detecting and preventing errors made within documents and forms that represent potential compliance risks. This results in proactive intervention, prevents errors, and improves customer satisfaction.

## The Amplification Effect

The impacts of AI agents for the bank's Compliance team include

- **Reduced processing time.** AI agents automate the manual tasks involved in regulatory compliance monitoring and reporting, such as data collection, aggregation, analysis, and report generation. This enables compliance professionals to focus on more strategic activities and reduces the overall processing time for compliance tasks.

- **Enhanced accuracy and consistency.** AI agents analyze vast amounts of data and identify patterns that may be missed by human reviewers. This leads to more accurate and consistent regulatory compliance assessments, reducing the risk of errors and omissions.

- **Improved timeliness of insights.** AI agents provide real-time insights into regulatory risks and compliance issues. Compliance professionals now proactively identify and address potential problems before they materialize, avoiding regulatory penalties and reputational damage.

- **Reduced regulatory compliance costs.** By off-loading compliance tasks to AI agents, the bank reduces the costs associated with regulatory compliance. This includes the costs of manual labor, software, and external consultants.

- **Enhanced regulatory risk mitigation.** AI agents help the compliance team identify and assess potential regulatory risks more effectively. This enables the compliance team to develop and implement mitigation strategies to reduce the likelihood of regulatory breaches.

- **Quantitative metrics.** Following are the metrics concerning AI agent amplification collected by the Compliance team. The range is reflective of each division's degree of readiness and specific workflows and processes.

| Measurement | The Amp Effect |
| --- | --- |
| Reduced processing time | 50%–70% |
| Enhanced accuracy and consistency | 85%–95% |
| Improved timeliness of insights | 60%–70% |
| Reduced regulatory compliance costs | 15%–25% |
| Enhanced regulatory risk mitigation | 15%–25% |

*The diverse ranges in this case study are due to the readiness of different divisions and the complexity and sophistication of their workflows and processes. Source: Ampliforce

AI agents streamline the bank's compliance processes, reduce costs, enhance its regulatory posture, and protect its ongoing reputation in the financial services industry.

# THE BOTTOM LINE

You've seen how a progressive company is reimagining work within its various divisions.

How can you implement a similar workforce transformation plan within your own business to achieve these kinds of Amplification Effects?

# APPENDIX 2:
# STRATEGIES OF INDUSTRY GIANTS TRANSFORMING BUSINESS AND REDEFINING WORK

The year 2024 marked the rapid adoption of AI agents by industry giants like JPMorgan, UnitedHealth Group, Visa, Mastercard, Toyota, and Siemens, underscoring a transformative shift in the global business landscape. This widespread implementation of AI technology at scale signifies a new era in how work is conducted and how knowledge is leveraged across various sectors. From fraud detection to health-care diagnostics, these agents are significantly reducing errors and improving operational efficiency, often by orders of magnitude. They're enabling hyper-personalized services in wealth management, health care, and customer service, breaking through limitations previously imposed by human capacity.

The ability of AI agents to learn and adapt in real time is pushing the boundaries of what's possible in areas like fraud prevention, cybersecurity, and manufacturing optimization. Moreover, AI is breaking down silos between different fields, as evidenced by Toyota's advanced materials research and Siemens's industrial metaverse.

The implications for the future of work are profound. Knowledge workers are increasingly becoming orchestrators and interpreters of AI-generated insights rather than primary data processors. This evolution demands new skills focused on AI collaboration, strategic interpretation of AI outputs, and ethical oversight of AI systems.

As AI agents become more sophisticated, the workplace is evolving into a hybrid environment where human creativity and judgment are amplified by AI's processing power and pattern-recognition abilities. This symbiosis between human and artificial intelligence is not just changing how work is done, but redefining what work is, promising unprecedented levels of productivity and innovation across industries. The future of work is here, and it's a collaborative dance between human ingenuity and artificial intelligence.

# FINANCIAL SERVICES

**JPMorgan**[1]

## WEALTH MANAGEMENT

- Objective: To provide personalized financial advice and improve investment strategies.

- Summary: JPMorgan has invested in AI for wealth management, enabling the analysis of vast amounts of data to offer tailored advice to clients. AI helps in predicting market trends, optimizing portfolios, and providing insights that enhance investment decisions.

- Before AI agents: Wealth managers relied heavily on manual analysis of market data and client information, limiting the depth and personalization of financial advice. The process was time consuming and prone to human biases.

- After AI agents: AI agents analyze massive datasets in real time, providing wealth managers with AI-driven insights for more personalized and data-backed investment strategies. This allows human advisors to focus on client relationships and complex decision-making.

# TRADE FINANCE AUTOMATION

- Objective: To streamline trade-finance operations and reduce manual intervention.

- Summary: AI is used to automate trade-finance processes, including document verification and transaction monitoring. This reduces processing times, minimizes errors, and enhances the efficiency of trade operations.

- Before AI agents: Trade finance involved extensive manual document review, lengthy verification processes, and time-consuming compliance checks, leading to slow transaction processing and increased risk of errors.

- After AI agents: AI agents automate document processing, conduct real-time compliance checks, and facilitate faster, more accurate trade-finance transactions. This allows human workers to focus on complex cases and relationship management.

## INVESTMENT ANALYTICS

- Objective: To enhance investment research and decision-making.

- Summary: AI-driven investment analytics provide deep insights into market trends and investment opportunities. AI models analyze large datasets to identify patterns and predict future movements, supporting more informed investment decisions.

- Before AI agents: Investment analysts spent significant time manually collecting and analyzing data from various sources, limiting the scope and speed of market insights.

- After AI agents: AI agents continuously analyze vast amounts of market data, identifying trends and opportunities that human analysts might miss. This allows human analysts to focus on strategic decision-making and interpreting AI-generated insights.

# INSURANCE

## UnitedHealth Group[2]

## CUSTOMER SERVICE AUTOMATION

- Objective: To improve customer interactions and streamline service processes.

- Summary: UnitedHealth Group is investing in AI to automate customer-service tasks and enhance patient interactions.

- Before AI agents: Customer service relied heavily on human agents handling a high volume of repetitive queries, leading to long wait times, inconsistent responses, and limited availability outside business hours.

- After AI agents: AI agents now handle routine customer inquiries, using natural language processing to understand and respond to customer questions accurately and quickly. They can access vast amounts of information instantly, provide consistent responses, and are available 24/7. This allows human agents to focus on complex issues that require empathy and nuanced understanding, improving overall customer satisfaction and operational efficiency.

## CALL DOCUMENTATION AND SUMMARIZATION

- Objective: To expedite call documentation and improve the accuracy of customer interaction summaries.

- Summary: UnitedHealth Group is using AI and natural language processing to rapidly generate accurate summaries of consumer interactions with their contact centers.

- Before AI agents: Call-center agents spent significant time after each call manually documenting the interaction, leading to potential inaccuracies, inconsistencies, and reduced productivity.

- After AI agents: AI agents now automatically generate summaries of customer interactions in real time. They can accurately capture key points, action items, and relevant details from the conversation, saving millions of dollars in administrative work. This allows human agents to focus more on the actual customer interaction rather than post-call documentation, improving both efficiency and the quality of customer service.

## OPERATIONAL EFFICIENCY ENHANCEMENT

- Objective: To streamline internal processes and reduce administrative costs.

- Summary: UnitedHealth Group is leveraging AI to drive operational efficiencies and enhance the overall customer experience.

- Before AI agents: Many internal processes were manual and time consuming, involving data entry, document processing, and information retrieval from multiple systems. This led to inefficiencies, errors, and higher administrative costs.

- After AI agents: AI agents now automate many back-office processes, from claims processing to policy administration. They can extract information from various documents, cross-reference data across multiple systems, and perform complex calculations quickly and accurately. This not only reduces operational costs but also improves the speed and accuracy of services provided to customers.

## DATA ANALYSIS FOR PERSONALIZED HEALTH CARE

- Objective: To leverage vast amounts of health-care data for improved patient outcomes and personalized care.

- Summary: UnitedHealth Group is using AI to analyze large volumes of health-care data to identify trends, predict patient needs, and personalize care recommendations.

- Before AI agents: Analyzing health-care data was a time-consuming process that often relied on periodic reviews and limited datasets. This made it challenging to identify trends or make personalized recommendations in a timely manner.

- After AI agents: AI agents now continuously analyze vast amounts of health-care data in real time. They can identify patterns, predict potential health issues, and generate personalized care recommendations. This allows health-care providers to intervene proactively and tailor treatments more effectively, potentially improving patient outcomes and reducing health-care costs.

## FRAUD DETECTION AND PREVENTION

- Objective: To enhance the detection and prevention of fraudulent insurance claims.

- Summary: While not explicitly mentioned in the document, it's a common use case in the insurance industry and aligns with UnitedHealth's focus on operational efficiency and cost reduction.

- Before AI agents: Fraud detection often relied on rule-based systems and manual reviews, which were time consuming and could miss sophisticated fraud patterns.

- After AI agents: AI agents now use advanced machine learning algorithms to analyze claims data in real time, identifying potential fraud patterns that might be missed by traditional methods. They can adapt to new fraud tactics quickly, reducing financial losses and improving the integrity of the insurance system.

# PAYMENTS

**Visa**[3]

## FRAUD PREVENTION

- Objective: Enhance security and reduce fraudulent activities.

- Summary: Visa launched three new AI-powered tools in March 2024 to target remote transactions, non–Visa card payments, and real-time payments. These tools significantly improved fraud detection capabilities, enabling Visa to block $40 billion in fraudulent activity last year—nearly double the previous year's amount.

- Before AI agents: Fraud prevention relied heavily on rule-based systems and manual review of flagged transactions, leading to slower response times and higher false-positive rates. Human analysts spent significant time sifting through alerts, often missing subtle patterns of fraud due to the overwhelming volume of data.

- After AI agents: AI agents now analyze vast amounts of transaction data in real time, using advanced AI algorithms to detect and prevent fraud with greater accuracy and speed. They can identify complex fraud patterns that may be missed by human analysts, enhancing fraud detection capabilities by up to 80 percent. Human fraud analysts now focus on investigating complex cases, refining fraud-prevention strategies, and making high-level decisions based on AI-generated insights.

## INTERNAL EFFICIENCY AND INNOVATION

- Objective: Improve internal operations, employee productivity, and drive innovation.

- Summary: Visa implemented a GPT-4 instance for employees in 2023 to explore Generative AI applications. This initiative aims to enhance internal engineering efficiency and overall employee productivity by automating various tasks and enabling innovative solutions.

- Before AI agents: Employees spent a significant portion of their time on repetitive tasks, manual data entry, and searching for information across various internal systems. Innovation efforts were often siloed and limited by human capacity to research, analyze, and test new ideas.

- After AI agents: AI agents powered by Generative AI now handle routine tasks, automate report generation, and provide quick answers to employee queries. They assist in the innovation process by rapidly analyzing market trends, generating and evaluating ideas, and even conducting preliminary feasibility studies. This frees up human workers to focus on strategic thinking, creative problem-solving, and innovation.

## Mastercard[4]

# ADVANCED FRAUD DETECTION

- Objective: To significantly enhance fraud-detection capabilities in an increasingly complex digital-payment landscape.

- Summary: Mastercard announced a Generative AI model called **Decision Intelligence Pro** in February 2024, capable of scanning 1 trillion data points to predict whether transactions are legitimate.

- Before AI agents: Fraud-detection systems were largely based on static rules and thresholds, requiring frequent manual updates and generating high false-positive rates. Analysts spent considerable time reviewing flagged transactions, often struggling to keep up with evolving fraud tactics.

- After AI agents: AI agents now employ advanced AI algorithms to analyze vast amounts of transaction data in real time, adapting to new fraud patterns automatically. They can boost fraud-detection rates by an average of 20 percent and up to 300 percent in some cases. Human analysts now focus on investigating the most complex cases and developing strategic fraud-prevention measures.

## CYBERSECURITY ENHANCEMENT

- Objective: To bolster Mastercard's cybersecurity capabilities through AI-driven solutions.

- Summary: Mastercard has been building out its cybersecurity portfolio through acquisitions, including the purchase of AI start-ups like Baffin Bay Networks, to enhance threat-protection capabilities.

- Before AI agents: Cybersecurity efforts were often reactive, relying on human analysts to monitor threats, investigate incidents, and update security measures. This approach struggled to keep pace with the rapidly evolving threat landscape.

- After AI agents: AI agents now continuously monitor network traffic, automatically detect and respond to threats, and even predict potential security risks before they materialize. They can analyze patterns across vast datasets to identify emerging threats and vulnerabilities, allowing human cybersecurity experts to focus on strategic planning and addressing the most sophisticated attacks.

# INDUSTRIALS

**Toyota**[5]

## FACTORY AUTOMATION & ROBOTICS

- Objective: To enhance manufacturing efficiency and productivity.

- Summary: Toyota has built on its manufacturing prowess with investments in factory automation and robotics, leveraging AI to optimize production processes.

- Before AI agents: Manufacturing processes relied heavily on human workers for assembly, quality control, and process optimization. This led to variability in production quality and efficiency, as well as potential safety risks in certain manufacturing environments.

- After AI agents: AI agents now assist in various aspects of the manufacturing process, from optimizing assembly line operations to predictive maintenance of equipment. They analyze real-time data from sensors and machines to identify inefficiencies and potential issues before they occur, allowing human workers to focus on complex problem-solving and strategic process improvements.

## ADVANCED MATERIALS RESEARCH

- Objective: To accelerate the development of new materials for automotive applications.

- Summary: Toyota Ventures has invested in AI-driven advanced materials research, aiming to discover and develop new materials with enhanced properties for use in vehicle manufacturing.

- Before AI agents: Materials research was a time-consuming process that relied heavily on trial and error, with researchers manually testing various combinations and properties.

- After AI agents: AI agents now use AI algorithms to simulate and predict material properties, significantly speeding up the research process. They can analyze vast databases of material information to suggest novel combinations and structures, allowing human researchers to focus on validating the most promising candidates and applying them to real-world automotive challenges.

## HUMAN INTERACTIVE DRIVING

- Objective: To improve driver and vehicle safety through AI-enhanced autonomy features.

- Summary: Toyota Research Institute (TRI) is focusing on "Human Interactive Driving" as one of its core research areas, aiming to develop AI systems that can enhance driver safety without fully replacing human control.

- Before AI agents: Driver assistance systems were limited in their ability to adapt to complex driving situations and often required significant driver intervention.

- After AI agents: AI agents now power advanced driver assistance systems that can analyze road conditions, predict potential hazards, and provide real-time guidance to drivers. They learn from vast amounts of driving data to continually improve their performance, allowing human drivers to benefit from AI-enhanced safety features while maintaining control of the vehicle.

### Siemens[6]

## AI-DRIVEN DIGITAL TWINS

- Objective: To further industrial automation with AI-driven digital twins.

- Summary: Siemens has partnered with Nvidia to develop an "industrial metaverse" platform that enables more realistic, real-time virtual models of physical manufacturing environments.

- Before AI agents: Creating and maintaining digital models of manufacturing processes was labor intensive and often failed to capture the full complexity of real-world operations. Simulations were limited in their ability to predict and optimize performance.

- After AI agents: AI agents now power sophisticated digital twins that can simulate and optimize manufacturing processes in real time. They continuously update these models based on data from the physical world, allowing human engineers to test scenarios, identify bottlenecks, and optimize processes virtually before implementing changes in the real world.

# SIEMENS INDUSTRIAL COPILOT

- Objective: To develop AI-powered assistants for manufacturing workers.

- Summary: Siemens has collaborated with Microsoft to develop the Siemens Industrial Copilot, an AI assistant designed to support manufacturing workers across various industries.

- Before AI agents: Manufacturing workers often had to rely on their own experience and limited access to information when making decisions or troubleshooting issues on the factory floor.

- After AI agents: AI agents in the form of AI copilots now provide real-time assistance to human workers, offering instant access to relevant information, suggesting solutions to problems, and even predicting potential issues before they occur. This allows human workers to make more informed decisions and focus on complex tasks that require human judgment and creativity.

# GENERATIVE AI FOR INDUSTRIAL COMPANIES

- Objective: To bring Generative AI capabilities to industrial companies of all sizes.

- Summary: Siemens has partnered with Amazon Web Services (AWS) to integrate Amazon Bedrock, a service offering foundation models from leading AI companies, into Siemens's Mendix low-code development platform.

- Before AI agents: Developing and implementing AI solutions in industrial settings often required significant expertise and resources, limiting adoption, especially among smaller companies.

- After AI agents: AI agents powered by Generative AI can now assist in various aspects of industrial operations, from generating code for automation systems to creating documentation and analyzing complex datasets. This democratizes access to AI capabilities, allowing companies of all sizes to leverage advanced AI tools to improve their operations and decision-making processes.

# NOTES

## INTRODUCTION

1. Michael Chiu et al., "The Economic Potential of Generative AI: The Next Productivity Frontier," McKinsey & Company, June 2023, https://www.mckinsey.com/capabilities/mckinsey-digital/our-insights/the-economic-potential-of-generative-ai-the-next-productivity-frontier#introduction.

2. Chiu, "The Economic Potential."

3. *Automation in the Workplace*, Smartsheet, 2017, https://www.smartsheet.com/2017-automation-report.

## CHAPTER 1

1. "Hybrid Work Is Just Work. Are We Doing It Wrong?" Microsoft Work Trend Index, September 2022, https://www.microsoft.com/en-us/worklab/work-trend-index/hybrid-work-is-just-work.

2. "Hybrid Work."

3. "Hybrid Work."

4. Gallup, *State of the Global Workplace: 2023 Report*, https://www.gallup.com/workplace/349484/state-of-the-global-workplace.aspx#ite-506897.

5. Gallup, *State of the Global Workplace*.

6. Michael Campion and Emily Campion, "Research: When New IT Systems Shift the Burden onto Employees," *Harvard Business Review*, February 15, 2021, https://hbr.org/2021/02/research-when-new-it-systems-shift-the-burden-onto-employees.

7. *Automation in the Workplace*, Smartsheet, 2017, https://www.smartsheet.com/2017-automation-report.

8. "2024 Gen Z and Millennial Survey: Living and Working with Purpose in a Transforming World," Deloitte, 2024, https://www.deloitte.com/global/en/issues/work/content/genzmillennialsurvey.html.

9. Jonathan Vespa, "The Graying of America: More Older Kids by 2035," United States Census Bureau, March 13, 2018, https://www.census.gov/library/stories/2018/03/graying-america.html.

10. Anthony Klotz and Mark Bolino, "When Quiet Quitting Is Worse Than the Real Thing," *Harvard Business Review*, September 15, 2022, https://hbr.org/2022/09/when-quiet-quitting-is-worse-than-the-real-thing.

11. Gallup, *State of the Global Workplace*.

## CHAPTER 2

1. Ee Ning Foo, "The White-Collar Struggle for Productivity in the Information Age," *The Economics Review*, April 24, 2019, https://theeconreview.com/2019/04/24/the-white-collar-struggle-productivity-in-the-information-age/.

2. Ning Foo, "The White-Collar Struggle."

3. "The Anatomy of Work Global Index," Asana, 2023, https://asana.com/resources/anatomy-of-work.

4. *Automation in the Workplace*, Smartsheet, 2017, https://www.smartsheet.com/2017-automation-report.

5. Michael Chui et al., "The Social Economy: Unlocking Value and Productivity through Social Technologies," McKinsey Global Institute, July 1, 2012, https://www.mckinsey.com/industries/technology-media-and-telecommunications/our-insights/the-social-economy.

6. "Hybrid Work Is Just Work. Are We Doing It Wrong?" Microsoft Work Trend Index, September 2022, https://www.microsoft.com/en-us/worklab/work-trend-index/hybrid-work-is-just-work.

7. "Hybrid Work Is Just Work."

8. Daniel Tawfik et al., "Physician Burnout, Well-Being, and Work Unit Safety Grades in Relationship to Reported Medical Errors," *Mayo Clinic Proceedings* 93, no. 11 (2018): 1571–80, https://www.ncbi.nlm.nih.gov/pmc/articles/PMC6258067/.

9. David Scheinker et al., "Reducing Administrative Costs in US Health Care: Assessing Single Payer and Its Alternatives," *Health Services Research* 56, no. 4 (August 2021): 615–25; Tawfik et al., "Physician Burnout."

10. Tawfik et al., "Physician Burnout."

11. Edward Yardeni, "Productivity Is Making a Comeback," Yardeni Quick Takes, November 2, 2023, https://www.yardeniquicktakes.com/productivity-is-making-a-comeback/.

12. "Ed Yardini Sees 'Roaring 2020s' Scenario for US Economy," Bloomberg News, July 24, 2023, https://www.bloomberg.com/news/videos/2023-07-24/ed-yardeni-sees-roaring-2020s-scenario-for-us-economy-video.

# CHAPTER 4

1. Abraham Zaleznik, "The 'Hawthorne Effect,'" Baker Library Historical Collections, Harvard Business School, 1984, https://www.library.hbs.edu/hc/hawthorne/09.html.

2. Richard Stevenson, "85 Compliance Statistics You Need to Know in 2023," Drata Research, July 14, 2023, https://drata.com/blog/compliance-statistics.

3. *State of Compliance Trends Report 2023*, NorthRow, 2023, https://www.northrow.com/blog/compliance-in-2023-report.

4. Samantha Regan, Jessica McDermott, and Anne Godbold, "Can Compliance Keep up with Warp-Speed Change?," Accenture, May 18, 2022, https://www.accenture.com/us-en/insights/consulting/compliance-risk-study.

5. Rob Shelton and David Percival, *Breakthrough Innovation and Growth*, PwC, September 2013, https://www.pwc.es/es/publicaciones/gestion-empresarial/assets/breakthrough-innovation-growth.pdf.

6. Shelton and Percival, *Breakthrough Innovation and Growth*.

7. Michael Chui et al., *McKinsey Technology Trends Outlook 2023*, McKinsey & Company, July 20, 2023, https://www.mckinsey.com/capabilities/mckinsey-digital/our-insights/the-top-trends-in-tech.

8. Shelton and Percival, *Breakthrough Innovation and Growth*.

9. Daniella Seiler and Heather Hanselman, *McKinsey Global Surveys, 2021: A Year in Review*, McKinsey & Company, December 2021, https://www.mckinsey.com/~/media/mckinsey/featured%20insights/mckinsey%20global%20surveys/mckinsey-global-surveys-2021-a-year-in-review.pdf.

## CHAPTER 6

1. Ellyn Shook and Paul Daugherty, *Work, Workforce, Workers Reinvented in the Age of Generative AI*, 2024, https://www.accenture.com/content/dam/accenture/final/accenture-com/document-2/Accenture-Work-Can-Become-Era-Generative-AI.pdf.

2. Martin Baily and Aidan Kane, "How Will AI Affect Productivity?," Brookings, May 2, 2024, https://www.brookings.edu/articles/how-will-ai-affect-productivity/.

3. Tim Fountaine, Brian McCarthy, and Tamim Saleh, "Building the AI-Powered Organization," *Harvard Business Review*, July/August 2019, https://hbr.org/2019/07/building-the-ai-powered-organization.

4. Fountaine, McCarthy, and Saleh, "Building the AI-Powered Organization."

5. Raman Deol, "Is the AI Hype Translating to AI Jobs?" Deel, October 31, 2023, https://www.deel.com/blog/ai-hype-ai-jobs/.

6. Gartner, "U.S. Employees' Willingness to Go Above and Beyond at Work Hits Three-Year Low, According to Gartner," press release, September 11, 2018, https://www.gartner.com/en/newsroom/press-releases/2018-09-11-us-employees-willingness-to-go-above-and-beyond-at-work-hits-three-year-low-according-to-gartner.

7. Lauren Park, Katherine Gibbard, and Lin Grensing-Pophal, "Upskilling Your Workforce for the AI Era," SAP, last updated March 20, 2024, https://www.sap.com/insights/viewpoints/upskilling-your-workforce-for-the-ai-era.html.

8. "How to Reskill Your Workforce in the Age of AI," *Harvard Business Review*, August 25, 2023, https://hbr.org/2023/08/how-to-reskill-your-workforce-in-the-age-of-ai.

9. "How to Reskill."

10. "How to Reskill"; Park, Gibbard, and Grensing-Pophal, "Upskilling."

11. "How to Reskill."

12. "How to Reskill"; Park, Gibbard, and Grensing-Pophal, "Upskilling."

13. John Caplan, "Why Businesses Need to Prioritize Upskilling and Reskilling to Stay Competitive," *Forbes*, July 15, 2021, https://www.forbes.com/sites/johncaplan/2021/07/15/why-businesses-need-to-prioritize-upskilling-and-reskilling-to-stay-competitive/; Jorge Tamayo et al., "Reskilling in the Age of AI," *Harvard Business Review*, Sep/Oct 2023, https://hbr.org/2023/09/reskilling-in-the-age-of-ai.

14. Tamayo, "Reskilling."

15. Mcdonald's, *McDonald's Archway to Opportunity Progress Report*, https://www.archwaystoopportunity.com/ProgressReport.pdf; McDonald's; "McDonald's Unveils New Archways to Careers Mobile App for Restaurant Employees," press release, January 22, 2020, https://corporate.mcdonalds.com/corpmcd/our-stories/article/new-employee-app.html; McDonald's, "Our Big Bet: Investing in Education Pathways for Restaurant Employees," press release, March 29, 2018, https://corporate.mcdonalds.com/corpmcd/our-stories/article/education_pathways.html.

# EPILOGUE

1. Ryan Browne, "Elon Musk Says AI Will Eventually Create a Situation Where 'No Job Is Needed,'" *CNBC*, November 2, 2023, https://www.cnbc.com/2023/11/02/tesla-boss-elon-musk-says-ai-will-create-situation-where-no-job-is-needed.html.

# APPENDIX 2

1. CB Insights, *AI Strategies for 11 of the World's Largest Companies* (May 2024), 5.

2. CB Insights, AI *Strategies*, 22.

3. CB Insights, AI Strategies, 12.

4. CB Insights, AI Strategies, 17.

5. CB Insights, AI Strategies, 58.

6. CB Insights, AI Strategies, 64.

# ABOUT THE AUTHOR

**MARCO BUCHBINDER** is CEO of Ampliforce, an artificial intelligence firm. By deploying AI agents to handle tedious manual tasks so humans can focus on more impactful roles, Ampliforce improves organizational productivity while increasing job satisfaction and retention.

Prior to Ampliforce, Marco spent eighteen years at EMC Corporation, a $23 billion cloud computing, storage, and big data firm, holding roles in general management, strategic planning, sales management, and M&A. Before that, he served as President & COO of GuestMetrics, an analytics provider focused on the hospitality industry, and as CEO of Technogym North America, a world leader in fitness and digital wellness solutions. Marco has also held leadership roles in two start-ups acquired by Fortune 500 companies: Storability Software (now part of Oracle [NASDAQ: ORCL]) and Advanced Solutions (now part of Waste Management).

A global citizen, Marco has held five international assignments (Milan, Rome, Vienna, Buenos Aires, and London), has personally implemented and been a board member of several international joint ventures (in Mexico, Brazil, UK, Egypt, India, Japan, and China), and speaks four languages.

He earned a bachelor's degree in political science with a concentration in international business from Boston College and has participated in a number of executive education programs, including courses at London Business School and Harvard Business School.

Made in the USA
Middletown, DE
29 September 2024

61672645R00113